R. C. J[illegible]

The Shaping of Foreign Policy

THE SHAPING OF FOREIGN POLICY

The Role of the Secretary of State as Seen by Dean Acheson

by **RONALD J. STUPAK**

Miami University

THE ODYSSEY PRESS

Published by The Odyssey Press,
a division of Western Publishing Company, Inc.

Printed in the United States
Library of Congress Catalog Card Number: 77-92591
A 0 9 8 7 6 5 4 3 2 1

ACKNOWLEDGMENTS

The author is grateful to the following writers, publishers, and literary agents for permission to use the materials listed below:

Alexander DeConde: *The American Secretary of State: An Interpretation.* New York: Frederick A. Praeger, Inc., 1962. Reprinted with permission of the publisher.

Walter Millis, Harvey C. Mansfield, and Harold Stein: *Arms and the State: Civil-Military Elements in National Policy.* New York: The Twentieth Century Fund, Inc., 1958. Reprinted with permission of the publisher.

The research for this book was undertaken while the author was a Fellow of the Mershon Center for Education in National Security.

To my Mother and Father—and Valeska

Foreword

Dr. Stupak's book appears in print almost exactly twenty years after Dean Acheson entered upon his eventful term as the senior member of President Truman's Cabinet. Secretaries of the federal departments are not ordinarily engaging figures for biographies, much less for specialized studies of their perspectives on policy and their strategies as inventive politicians. When a Cabinet Secretary attracts the attention of a political scientist, it is as likely to be for the party, electoral, or legislative periods of his career as it is for his administration of one of the major departments. Cabinet members usually derive their principal usefulness, and hence their appointments, from their symbolic contributions to a President's coalition. Because a President's coalition continuously forms and reforms, tenure in a Cabinet-level post is often short, and opportunities for seizing political control and giving policy direction to a large department are usually fleeting. Few Cabinet officers have had the clear Presidential instructions, strong personal inclinations, and well-developed skills of Robert Strange McNamara, who recently mastered and disciplined one of the great departments with notable energy and fame.

Secretary Acheson was the truly memorable figure of Harry Truman's Administration. If only for his impeccable style and personal appearance—biting wit, mustache, homburg, and tweeds—he would be remembered largely, if not exclusively, by the legions of professional politicians and gossipy Washington personality watchers. But his significance surpasses these trivial if arresting details. He may well have been the most imposing Cabinet official from Franklin Roosevelt's third term through Eisenhower's second, that is, from 1941 to 1960.

Among his colleagues in Harry Truman's Cabinet from 1949 to 1953, who is remembered now? James V. Forrestal, the tragic figure of Pentagon reorganization, resigned barely two months after Inauguration Day. General George C. Marshall returned from retirement to serve briefly as Secretary of Defense after the outbreak of the Korean War. How many can recall the names of Mr. Truman's Secretaries of the Treasury, Commerce, Interior, Labor, or Agriculture, or that of his Attorney General, during the second term, without recourse to a reference shelf? If two decades' distance obscures the names of John W. Snyder, Charles Sawyer, Howard McGrath, and others, Dean Acheson's name remains prominent, and time has enhanced his reputation for diplomacy and departmental leadership. His formulation of national policy, in terms of both content and procedure, decisively shaped the use of American power at the outset of the Cold War. For all the partisan rhetoric surrounding the Dulles years, much of Achesonian doctrine remained the core of United States foreign policy throughout the 1950's, and in the late 1960's Acheson's influence has not passed from the theory and practice of his successors. He was among those who recommended Dean Rusk as Secretary of State to John F. Kennedy, and as a consultant he served both Kennedy and Lyndon Johnson on special missions.

Ronald Stupak, as a political scientist, has judiciously staked out two particularly important and, I think, subtle aspects of Acheson's biography. He has elected to reconstruct the Secretary of State's *perspectives* on foreign policy—that is, the *expectations* he held for his country's future and for that of the global system of nations; the *identifications* he had with interests, institutions, and ideas, both personally and as Secretary; and the *demands* he made on his nation's behalf, as its chief diplomat. In addition, Stupak has analyzed with uncommon explicitness Mr. Acheson's *strategies*, that is, means for using his available resources in the arenas of Presidential policy making, legislative-executive relations, public opinion, and foreign offices of allies and adversaries. He has wisely left to historians and biographers, upon the fulfillment of Mr. Acheson's contributions to his country, the investigation of the sources of his perspectives and the motivations underlying his strategies. Happily, those contributions are not yet concluded, but the record, if explored thoroughly, already reveals a great deal about an extraordinary public figure.

Mr. Acheson's perspectives, as Professor Stupak's reconstruction indicates, include expectations that are realistic but open, and without tragic anticipations of his or his nation's role. His identifications are with diplomatic professionalism, not party politics; with traditional American participation in European affairs, rather than with the "underdeveloped" world of Asia; and with the Department of State, Foreign Service, and Presidency rather than with Congress, public opinion, or specialized interest groups. His demands emphasize distinctiveness, "class," "finesse," and skill in the exercise of diplomatic arts. Whether in crises or routine situations, Acheson's fundamental perspectives have varied little.

Acheson's expectations concerning the present and future of international relations are founded on the very high probability of the maintenance of the nation-state as the chief unit of world diplomacy. Although he was instrumental in strengthening the General Assembly through the Uniting for Peace Resolution, the United Nations occupies a secondary place in Acheson's assessment of important arenas for inter-nation action. What is more, he has not postulated the likelihood of, or hopefulness for, the establishment of world organizations having powers that supercede national prerogatives. He served his secretaryship before the exponential increase of nations through the admission of new states to sovereignty and the consequent doubling of United Nations membership. Further, Acheson's anticipated future is, nevertheless, relatively open; at least, it remains free of any assumption of inevitable war or of the probability of world Communist domination. To avoid war and stem Communist hegemony, Acheson expects continued reliance on force as an instrument of American policy. He does not shrink from the military implications of his expectations about the likely power arrangements among nations. Associated with this perspective was, and is, a recognition of the continuing struggle among human beings, organized in nations; of the ineradicability of conflict; and of the virtues of realistic, professional norms for managing and affecting the world struggle. These expectations are bound to a distinctly historical view of diplomatic events. Acheson places himself and his client-nation, the United States, in the grand diplomatic tradition shaped by slowly changing national demands. Hence, he can fit Soviet Communism to the pattern of Russian national objectives antedating the 1917 Revolution, and he can imagine the world arena as one occupied by professional diplomats dealing with issues that are largely impervious to sudden dramatic alterations by modern social-scientific or peace-research-oriented initiatives. Likewise, he adheres to a preference for step-by-step, incremental response to events over comprehensive theoretical planning and scheming.

Dr. Stupak's efforts to derive Mr. Acheson's essential expectations may at first glance to some readers appear rather artificial, too schematic, and overly simplified. This risk is especially apparent when working with the public statements of so stylish a spokesman as Dean Acheson, who has framed his philosophy in articulate and eloquent periods. Yet this selective codification of Achesonianism clearly transcends the obvious and commonplace when one compares Acheson's expectations with those of, say, John Foster Dulles, his successor, or with those of contemporary critics of the character of U.S. foreign policy, say, Senators Eugene McCarthy or J. W. Fulbright. With both these sources of foreign-policy alternatives, Dean Acheson, Dean Rusk, and Lyndon Johnson clearly have been at odds. On the one hand, Mr. Dulles believed world affairs and America's role to be subject to moral appraisal not unlike the ethical judgments required in relations among individuals or within nations. Mr. Dulles expected the Soviet Union's actions to be dictated more by Communist ideology than by historic Russian demands or conceptions of short-run interest. On the other hand, Acheson's protagonists within the Democratic Party expect the United Nations to be capable of a more constructive role in world affairs and of a more promising basis for global institution-building. Some expect force to have less influence and anticipate greater limits on the efficacy of national power. Some also believe in the capacity of aroused and demonstrative publics to be at once well informed and influential.

From Acheson's expectations one can better understand his identification with national sovereignty, European unifying tendencies, and the enhancement of American power and, hence, influence throughout the world. In the domestic arena, Acheson identified with the interests of his employer, the President. Foreign policy, according to his conception, is the Executive's foreign policies, and Congress is to be regarded as a sometimes helpful critic, an occasionally useful political ally, but a rare source of innovation. Likewise, the opinion of various elites and groups among the broad public must be informed to support the Executive, but "public opinion" itself is not to be relied on as the source of inspiration in formulating and applying policy.

These expectations about the future and identifications with his peers mark the distinctive character of Secretary Acheson. His style, personally and officially, is further revealed by certain evident demands that he has made on himself and others. Personal power appears not to have been a passion; he never sought elective office, he once resigned from the Treasury over a policy dispute, and he administered his Department without any apparent excessive domination of his colleagues for domination's sake. Legal success earned him personal wealth, but the enrichment of his private portfolio could not have consumed him, for he devoted the prime years of his life to public service. Acheson seems to have valued the exercise and perfecting of skill—in law, in diplomacy, in writing. His legal skill brought him to government, his diplomatic finesse won him high appointive office, and in retirement he wrote frequently and variously, always with wit and force. But craftmanship alone was not an object of desire and admiration on his part. Loyalty to church, college, and country, to his President and to his friends, characterized his career. Great successes flowed from his fidelity to President Truman; great troubles followed upon his unwillingness to turn his back on a former associate, Alger Hiss, in disrepute. Likewise, his conception of self and his obvious demand for esteem resulted in mixed effects. His elegant appearance and eloquent speech attracted the admiration of some and drew the ridicule of others. His learned discourses before Congress delighted his fellow Democrats, but his sharp rebuttals inflamed his Republican antagonists.

Yet these traits combined to form a remarkably strong as well as striking figure. Hence, when Harry Truman, the professional politician from Independence, Missouri, asked Dean Acheson, the sometime diplomat and lawyer's lawyer from Middletown, Connecticut, to be his Secretary of State, the latter imported several assets to his office. His base of power was founded on his intimate relationship with and respect for the President, and he adhered to some well-defined strategies in protecting and enhancing this source of power. Similarly, Acheson relied on the diplomatic skills of his Department to support him in both domestic and world affairs. Unlike Dulles, Acheson was both leader and representative of his Department. Originally, he brought to office intimate knowledge of Congress and its foreign-policy leaders: having been previously charged with directing the Department's liaison with Congress, Acheson enjoyed an initially favorable reputation with Senate and House leaders that he converted into influence with them when he was Secretary. In addition to these power bases, he also enjoyed the respect of European diplomats that he had earned in previous foreign service. Besides the usual knowledge one associates with a Secretary, Acheson was experienced in international finance, and he understood the military elements of foreign policy as had few predecessors.

To take advantage of these assets, Acheson's strategies, as Stupak reconstructs them, were quite explicit. To maintain and use his special relationship with President Truman, the Secretary of State defended intrusions on executive power, acted as the President's principal source of foreign-policy information, established himself as the chief foreign-affairs adviser to the White House, introduced himself into the writing of Presidential speeches, protected the President from inflexible over-institutionalization of policy-making processes, jealously guarded his own itinerary against absences from Washington, and secured access to the President's right hand.

To strengthen and deploy the State Department's power over foreign policy, Acheson maintained informal but regular contacts with other departments concerned with external affairs, especially the Department of Defense. He insisted on giving initiative to State Department policy at the earliest stages of development. In this characteristic, he foreshadowed the active leadership of Robert McNamara in the Pentagon. And he involved himself in crisis decisions when precedents were set that would affect long-term, evolutionary planning. Through this display of senior executive leadership, he bolstered the morale and esprit of the Department. By rewarding talent and ridiculing mediocrity he attracted, retained, and promoted colleagues who supplemented his personal capacities with greater organizational productivity.

With Congress, Acheson vigorously advocated executive supremacy in foreign relations but assiduously cultivated informal contacts with leaders, carefully informed relevant committees, and especially appreciated the growing involvement of the House of Representatives in foreign affairs. Specifically, he saw the possibility and potentiality of drawing the House Foreign Affairs Committee into coalition against the somewhat more independent Senate Foreign Relations Committee. Thus, the legislative branch afforded public support as well as criticism of his and Mr. Truman's foreign policies.

Among public opinion elites he relied on the Council on Foreign Relations, the Foreign Policy Association, and similar small, specialized, but well-informed groups to build support for his ideas throughout the country.

The outcomes and effects of Acheson's use of his resources must be accounted mixed. As Under Secretary and Secretary he unquestionably initiated new policies—among them the Greek-

Turkish Aid Program, European Economic Recovery, the North Atlantic Treaty Organization, the Uniting for Peace Resolution in the United Nations, and the defense of Korea. Near the end of his term, however, he was a campaign issue, of negative partisan value to his President and to his party's 1952 Presidential candidate. In retrospect, most, though not all, appraisers now regard his policy initiatives as positive contributions to national security and world peace. The foundations of European recovery were established. The threats of Soviet advance in Western Europe were thwarted. The reconciliation of Eastern and Western Europe was anticipated. The beginnings of aid to underdeveloped areas were made. And the advancement of Chinese Communism was contained. All these Cold War achievements have helped to avert nuclear confrontation.

Time has, in other words, dealt kindly with Dean Acheson. A party liability in 1952, he became, after retirement from the law, a consultant to John Kennedy, a confidant to Lyndon Johnson, and a special emissary of both. His stewardship of the first department of government remains a model for his successors, always to study, often to emulate, now and then to amend or avoid.

Advocates of "the New Politics" now challenge many of Acheson's precepts. Some historians of "the New Left" marshall evidence to establish the culpability of the United States in starting the Cold War, theorists of world politics emphasize the roles of "the third world" and of the "underdeveloped" nations in international relations, and the merits of Presidential dominance in the conduct of foreign policy currently undergo reexamination by some domestic liberals.

Whatever the outcome of the reappraisal of American foreign policy in the post-war years, Ronald Stupak's book presents a model for the study of the perspectives and the strategies of other administrator-diplomatists. Such studies promise both to depict varying elements of stability and fluctuation in national diplomatic conduct and to reveal alternative ways of conducting the external relations of the United States in the turbulent present and uncertain future.

JAMES A. ROBINSON
Director
Mershon Center for
Education in National Security

Contents

Introduction

This book is an attempt to construct an operational code for the Secretary of State in the American foreign-policy decision-making process after World War II, formulated from the perspective of a particular occupant of that office, Dean G. Acheson.

Operational code, throughout this book, is defined as those rules that Acheson believes to be essential for the effective performance of the Secretary of State in his role as a policy maker. It is not assumed that these rules apply exclusively to the office of the Secretary of State, as some of the principles have general applicability to other positions in public administration and business. Yet there are special characteristics of the office of the Secretary of State that give the overall operating framework unique importance as a guide to action for anyone in that office. Some of these distinct features, which are elaborated upon in the following chapters, include: (1) the almost total dependence of the Secretary of State upon the personality style of the President; (2) the absence of an interest group outside of the official governmental structure to support the Secretary before Congress and the President; (3) the overwhelming foreign-policy orientation of the organization that he heads; and (4) the political-diplomatic environment in which he must perform.

The operational code can be constructed by analyzing a web of interrelated functions that Mr. Acheson deems essential in the foreign-policy process. A combination of personal, institutional, and environmental elements are investigated by examining the writings of Mr. Acheson, writings and documents about Mr. Acheson, material on the office of the Secretary of State and American foreign policy in general, and interviews conducted with key personalities. The rules of the operational code are then abstracted to ascertain their adaptability for other Secretaries of State. The President–Secretary of State partnership pattern contained within the code is evaluated and contrasted with other more idealized relationships in the concluding chapter to see why the more idealized patterns are incompatible with Acheson's guide for Secretaries of State of today and tomorrow.

Another aim of this book is to evaluate the impact, both temporary and permanent, of a particular personality on a governmental institution's influence, objectives, functions, and organization. Finally, and most important, an effort is made to demonstrate how, in Acheson's view, the Secretary of State can achieve and maintain the role of chief Presidential adviser in the foreign-policy process.

In looking at the Secretary of State as viewed by Mr. Acheson, examination is made of inputs such as his personality prejudices;

his philosophical outlooks on life, politics, and his own definition of his role as a policy maker; his perception of the relationships within the institutional framework of the State Department; his views of the influences and pressures from competing decision-making units and personalities; and his concept of the role of indirect participants in the actual decision-making units.

In terms of output, an effort is made to identify, assess, and weigh Mr. Acheson's power and influence on the policy process by: (1) investigating his roles and contributions as an official in the Truman Administration on the assumption that his power was closely correlated with his position in an official hierarchy; (2) relying on well-placed judges and authorities who can assess his influence on the process; (3) studying his participation in specific decisions and policies in order to pierce the facade of formal position and reputation; and (4) weighing his influence on the output of policies which he championed in relationship to the influence that was wielded by other decision makers in the determination of final policy outcomes. Furthermore, by identifying the operational elements[1] and methods which Mr. Acheson maintains the Secretary must possess to reach a position of maximum influence in the foreign policy process, it is possible to see how a Secretary of State can accentuate his importance in that process.

Of course, an operational code cannot be judged in terms of being either true or false; it is only more or less academically enlightening or operationally productive and must, therefore, be judged by whether or not it helps to generalize more accurately about the political process or serves as a meaningful guide for others in similar positions.

By developing the Acheson operational code, it is hoped to

[1] *Operational elements,* as defined throughout this book, means those techniques and procedures that Mr. Acheson deems essential to the way a Secretary of State must perform his job.

avoid a fragmented study of foreign policy and the policy process by calling attention to the interrelationship of events, personalities, and organizations, as perceived by a participating actor who has been successful as a policy maker in, and influential as a policy adviser out of the formal process. That techniques and abstractions can never be ends in themselves, that policy ultimately depends on such additional inputs as personal motivation, institutional purpose, and the national and international environments, is, however, fully recognized.[2] All these elements are carefully investigated from Mr. Acheson's perspective.

Because today one "hears more discussion of the views of commentators and less discussion from the artists themselves,"[3] the concern of this book is with the use of power and the elaboration of its composition and manipulation in the policy-making process as interpreted by a professional. Though the search is for objectivity in the social sciences, this does not mean that one is required to "become a cybernetic machine" or to pursue the study of politics to the total exclusion of the subjective view.[4] Therefore, the development of an operational code by analysis of one decisional unit as seen by an active participant hopefully will add behavioral and operational dimensions to the many existing biographical and historical studies of the office of the Secretary of State.

Too many models and conceptual frameworks in political sci-

[2] Snyder and Paige, "The United States Decision to Resist Aggression in Korea: The Application of an Analytical Scheme," pp. 212–214.

[3] Acheson, *Morning and Noon*, p. 55.

[4] Acheson, *Power and Diplomacy*, pp. 136–137. In addition see Herbert C. Kelman, "Social-Psychological Approaches to the Study of International Relations: A Definition of Scope," *International Behavior: A Social-Psychological Analysis*, p. 14. "A recent focus for conceptualization and research in international politics has been the behavior of the individual actors who are involved in the formulation and execution of foreign policy."

ence have almost entirely ignored the individual personality; at best, the personality is seen only as an instrument, a voice, or a symbol. In practice, the powers of the Secretary of State are neither self-executing nor exercised by a committee, but are predominantly dependent upon the quality of one man. As McGeorge Bundy has pointed out, ". . . the man must make the office more often than not; no one can claim for the office of Secretary of State the peculiar dignity that invests the Supreme Court or the White House."[5] The nature of the Secretaryship is so flexible that the office becomes almost the creature of its occupant. Consequently, throughout the construction of Acheson's policy-making guide, there is an effort to focus on the complex interplay between his personality and the other elements of the Secretary of State's policy-making arena to detect both unique features and broader generalizations attending the office.

It is essential, at this juncture, to clarify what this book will not attempt to do. There will be no effort made to psychoanalyze Mr. Acheson in relation to his childhood, education, or family life, in order to explain why he views the role of the Secretary of State in the manner that he does. This is beyond the scope of this conceptualization and beyond the capabilities of the author. Acheson's operational code is not limited to the period when he was Secretary of State; a longer-range view is undertaken so that a more comprehensive investigation and candid interpretation may be made of Acheson's view of the office up to the present day. And this will not be an historical biography: rather it will be a systematic presentation of Acheson's perception of how a Secretary of State should function to maximize his policy-making role. Too many people have not understood or have drastically misunderstood what this man thinks and what this man has done. It is hoped that this book, using colorful episodes only to clarify cer-

[5] Bundy, *The Pattern of Responsibility,* p. 3. See also DeConde, *The Secretary of State: An Interpretation,* p. 38.

tain rules of the operational code, will help to set the record straight.

A key problem since the end of the Second World War has been to define the "proper" role of the Secretary of State in the foreign-policy process; there has been a simultaneous growth and decline of the Secretaryship. In an affirmative vein, the Secretary of State has emerged on the world scene as the most visible spokesman for United States diplomacy. His office has grown steadily in importance because of the vast increase in American foreign relations and the expansion of the power and influence of the Presidency itself. However, even if the postulate is granted that the Secretary of State should have primacy in advising on international policy, his role simply cannot be defined in formal, unambiguous terms. Faced by new problems and dimensions in the foreign-policy process—institutional proliferation, summit diplomacy, transformation of military methods—the Secretary as an individual has a key role in the policy process that he cannot avoid, just as America generally has a key role in world affairs that it cannot avoid. His position thus becomes a microcosm of the issues, pressures, and dilemmas that exist in both the functional and structural aspects of the policy-making arena in the United States today.

Therefore, before attempting to construct Acheson's operational code, an effort is made to describe and analyze the environment of the foreign-policy process of the United States since World War II. In this way, a broader, generalized picture of the challenges and opportunities presented to the Secretary of State as a policy maker can be developed. It can then be used as an undergirding for Acheson's more particularized view of how he believes a Secretary of State can best respond to these new phenomena.

It is the identification of Acheson with the policies of the

Truman Administration that give his insights into the policy process their most authoritative dimensions. He was instrumental in helping to recoup and retain the supremacy of civilian authority and the diplomatic method over the military and proposed military solutions to international problems, such as the Korean "total victory" campaign, at a time when the military dramas were much more visible than the diplomatic. He was strategic in such policy initiatives and innovations as "containment," the Marshall Plan, NATO, and the hydrogen bomb. He was a major participant in the formulation of the Korean decisions. He was a leader in the original formulation of plans for military deterrence. And he was a principle advocate of the "get tough" policy vis-à-vis the Soviet Union.[6]

His importance in the formulation of the foreign-policy programs of the Truman Administration is attested to by two of his former State Department colleagues, Paul H. Nitze and Theodore C. Achilles, who said in separate interviews:

It was the decision by Acheson in 1947 to face the Russians with American strength and to have the United States take the leadership of the West that was the turning point in American post-war policy and in the trend of the history of American foreign relations. His decision to make the change was the key decision in this matter. Others had been suggesting the same change and, in fact, had made it; however, Acheson was the supreme advocate who made this change final and pushed it into policy.[7]

Secretary of State Acheson was both an initiator of policy and a forceful advocate of those policies that he personally believed to be correct. He was an active rather than a passive policy maker.[8]

In effect, as an official policy maker, Acheson demonstrated the

[6] Truman, *Memoirs: Years of Trial and Hope;* Huntington, *The Common Defense,* p. 432.

[7] Interview with Paul H. Nitze, April 15, 1966 (paraphrased).

[8] Interview with Theodore C. Achilles, April 13, 1966 (paraphrased).

ability to operate in such a fashion that he was able not only to participate in, but many times able to direct and coordinate the flow of major policies and decisions.

An important phenomenon of American politics and of the policy-making process is that retired officials often are influential long after departing from their formal offices. The following item appeared in *Newsweek* magazine on April 25, 1966:

> Acheson radiates disdain for General de Gaulle and all his works. It is Acheson who has been the chief drafter of the notes and speeches that have gone into the Administration's extensive publicity campaign [to retain unity within NATO]. (p. 40)

Over the years Dean Acheson has been called a Washington, D.C., "high priest"; "the most powerful non-office holding critic and molder of United States foreign policy anywhere in the world"; the third-ranking outstanding Secretary of State in American history; and a Presidential "friend-consultant-adviser" of President Lyndon B. Johnson's "outer-inner" policy group.[9] There is no doubt that Acheson's influence on policy has been lasting and recognizable long after he has left the official policy-making family. Indeed, Acheson's influence supports James N. Rosenau's generalization that "probably the largest number of individual opinion-makers are those who carry into retirement a previously acquired positional prominence."[10] Furthermore, Acheson's continued influence on American foreign policy is supported in a number of the "personal histories" of the Kennedy administration that have recently been published.

The years of the Acheson Secretaryship were years of challenge, danger, and innovation in the international environment. What were the lasting effects of these revolutionary years on the American foreign-policy process? What were the unique and gen-

[9] Bagdikian, "The 'Inner, Inner Circle' Around Johnson."
[10] Rosenau, *Public Opinion and Foreign Policy*, p. 70.

eralizing tendencies in the role of the Secretary of State in the policy process and, particularly, in Dean Acheson's interpretation of this role? What are the generalizations about the Secretary's role in the policy-making process that can be abstracted from this particular operational code? These are the questions to which this book will be directed.

It is impossible to acknowledge all the various assistance given to me by professors, colleagues, and friends. My debt is so great to so many people that I will simply list the names of those who have assisted me in various ways beyond the normal call of duty: Ambassador Theodore C. Achilles (Ret.), Ambassador J. C. Satterthwaite (Ret.), Boyd Crawford, Carl Marcy, Paul H. Nitze, Pat Holt, John M. Vorys, Carlton Savage, Lawrence J. R. Herson, Louis Nemzer, Harvey C. Mansfield, Edwin H. Fedder, Gene E. Rainey, W. Andrew Axline, James N. Rosenau, Richard U. Sherman, Jr., and Mostafa Rejai.

I must record several special debts to those who gave me the help and encouragement I needed to complete this study: Dean G. Acheson, Professor Edgar S. Furniss, Jr., Mrs. Georgialee Furniss, and my wife, Dolores. The opportunity to talk to Mr. Acheson was especially rewarding: it gave me a chance to corroborate my library research and to get some insights that could only have been obtained from a personal discussion with such a candid personality.

And finally, it is with pleasure that I record my thanks to the Mershon Center for Education in National Security on the Ohio State University campus, and to its Director, James A. Robinson, for the financial assistance and editorial advice which eased many of my burdens in the completion of this book. Also, Ann Trupp and the secretarial staff of the Mershon Center along with John B. Whiton deserve special thanks for being able to read and type my numerous drafts.

CHAPTER ONE

The Foreign-Policy Process in the United States Since World War II

A tremendous expansion of problems and a dramatic increase in complexity have been interjected into the foreign-policy process in the United States since World War II. These reverberations within the policy-making system have been the products of such revolutionary postwar changes in the international arena as: (1) the transformed nature of the United States' world commitments due to the bipolar balance between Russia and America; (2) the policy precedents formulated during the period of bipolar confrontation; (3) the technological revolutions in the communication, transportation, and military fields; (4) the organizational and structural transfigurations in the international diplomatic process;

and (5) the dynamic nature of the decision-making process itself in producing change at the same time that it deals with international issues. Not only have these interrelated aspects of the postwar international environment shattered traditional American attitudes toward foreign affairs; they have also produced a series of adjustments and readjustments within the policy-making system of the government.

In attempting to absorb these shocks and to adjust to the changing nature of its role within a transformed world, the United States has met with both successes and failures. To draw up a balance sheet of "wins" and "losses" is not the purpose of this analysis; rather, it is to examine transformations in the world system to demonstrate what changes they have brought within the foreign-policy process. Then we can proceed to analyze the challenges and opportunities which resulting new relationships have presented to the Secretary of State in his role as a policy maker. For whether the Secretary can effectively participate in the formulation, the coordination, and the execution of foreign policies may well be a test not only of him as a person, but of the national system of political responsibility. Thus, before dealing specifically with Mr. Acheson's views and actions on the various problems faced by the Secretary of State or his operational code, a broader analysis will be undertaken of the Secretary's role in the post-World War II foreign-policy process.

Norman A. Graebner, in *Cold War Diplomacy: American Foreign Policy, 1945-1960* (Princeton, N.J.: Van Nostrand Company, Inc., 1962, p. 7), writes:

> For the American people the fifteen years from 1945 to 1960 comprised an original experience. Never before in a time of comparative peace were they so fully involved in world affairs.

In this statement, Mr. Graebner has identified one of the major changes that has come about for the United States in the Cold

War atmosphere. Peace for Americans became a relative phenomenon after the war; in other words, a period of peace in the Cold War context became a peace that constantly had to be worked at. Therefore, since it is the foundation upon which the other variables have overlapped and interrelated to produce this profoundly different environment in which the American foreign-policy machine has had to operate, the United States–Soviet Union confrontation and its impacts on the American foreign-policy process will be examined first.

The breakdown of the great coalition that existed during World War II between the Soviet Union and the Western Allies was the beginning of the postwar bipolar world. Many differences among the Allies had been subordinated during the war, but once the common enemy was defeated, the problems of peace brought to the surface differing conceptions of what paths should be followed. At the same time, the decline and, in some cases, the disappearance of the great empires of Western Europe, plus the demise of the Japanese Empire, brought the United States and the Soviet Union to the preeminence of world power. "The destruction of the military power of Germany and Japan removed the [historic] counterweights which had for many years balanced Russia and restrained its expansiveness."[1] In addition, the American power that had been instrumental in the defeat of the Axis powers underwent rapid reduction, for once the hostilities were over, the Americans were spontaneous and headlong in their eagerness to return to civilian life. So, as the war ended, United States policy makers were faced with: (1) the disintegration of Europe as a protective security barrier, (2) the power of an expansive Soviet Union, and (3) the domestic pressures for a policy of massive demobilization.

It was with the adoption of the Truman Doctrine in 1947 that

[1] Acheson, *A Democrat Looks at His Party*, p. 41.

the official policy makers consciously undertook to contain what they perceived as Soviet power thrusts throughout the world—with this particular decision, the Truman Administration effected a major turning point in American foreign relations and in the history of the world.[2] With the Truman Doctrine, the objective of the United States became the conscious, sustained containment of Russian power by restoring a balance of power in both Europe and Asia. President Truman, in the second volume of his memoirs, has remarked on the historical significance of the new policy:

> This [the Truman Doctrine] was, I believe, the turning point in America's foreign policy which now declared that wherever aggression, direct or indirect, threatened the peace, the security of the United States was involved. (p. 106)

The assumption of active leadership of the Western world through such policy initiatives as the Truman Doctrine, the Marshall Plan, and the North Atlantic Treaty has had a tremendous impact on the United States internal foreign-policy process. The sustained leadership and effort that have been put forth by the government and people of the United States since 1947 represent a revolution in American foreign policy and the acceptance of wholly new burdens and responsibilities. Never before, short of periods of all-out hostilities, have the international energies and potentials of the United States been so mobilized and so committed to a struggle during a time of relative peace. Large military budgets, a powerful military force-in-being, foreign-aid programs, alliance agreements, and limited warfare have all been accepted. In effect, the bipolar confrontation has created a forced interlocking of the political, economic, propaganda, educational, and military aspects of United States foreign policy.

[2] Jones, *The Fifteen Weeks,* pp. vii, 12; Bundy, *The Pattern of Responsibility,* pp. 139–140. For a challenge to this interpretation, see Alperovitz, *Atomic Diplomacy: Hiroshima and Potsdam*. In addition, see the "Revisionist Historians" and their interpretations of the Cold War period.

The need for the United States to blend its policies more closely with those of allied nations through organizations such as NATO, SEATO, and the OAS has magnified the many complications that are inherent in coalition diplomacy. While seeking to pursue its own national interests, the United States has, at the same time, been forced to maintain a degree of flexibility which allows it to incorporate, or at least take account of, the desires of its allies. This has led to the interjection of both a foreign and a historical dimension to the formulation of American foreign policies. As American policies have come to influence the course of events not only for the United States, but for many nations throughout the world, pressures on the internal American foreign-policy process and on individual policy makers have been magnified.

The sudden and dramatic emergence of new states, particularly in Africa and Asia, infused with a sense of nationalism, economic expectations, and social equality, has produced other major complications for the United States. The multiplication of states and their drives toward neutralism and self-sufficiency have led to foreign-policy innovations such as the Point Four Program, foreign aid, and the increased use of multilateral diplomacy within the international organization context. In addition, the relative weakness of the new states, coupled with Russian and Chinese expansionist desires, has pushed the Cold War competition directly into underdeveloped areas. President Truman vividly related the importance of the peaceful development of the new nations to American national security and to international stability when he reflected on the Point Four Program:

> The development of those areas had become one of the major elements of our foreign policy. . . . The program in action had the effect of disarming hostile propagandists and in discouraging the advance of both Communism and extreme nationalism. (*Memoirs,* Vol. II, pp. 333, 337)

The discovery and development of nuclear weapons capable of unlimited violence transformed the nature of modern warfare, reduced the geographical security of the United States, exposed the American homeland to the immediacy of widespread devastation, exacerbated civil-military relations, and ushered in a new scientific era in man's understanding of the forces of nature. The impact that nuclear power was to have on international relations in general and on the American foreign-policy process in particular clearly was seen by Truman as early as 1945, when he said:

> Never in history has society been confronted with a power so full of potential danger and at the same time so full of promise for the future of man and for the peace of the world.
>
> . . . the discovery with which we are dealing involves forces of nature too dangerous to fit into any of our usual concepts. . . . In international relations, as in domestic affairs, the release of atomic energy constitutes a force too revolutionary to consider in the framework of old ideas.[3]

The shrinkage of the world in terms of the relations among states and between any given state and its official representatives abroad has produced an immediacy that foreign affairs have never known before. From the demand for speed in decision-making has come a paradox for American policy makers: on the one hand, the need for quick action has caused many decisions to be made with insufficient information, while the increase of communicative interaction between states, the home offices, and the field offices has resulted in too much information, too much uncoordinated "noise," within the policy-making process.[4] Accompanying these technological and communicative improvements has been a vast increase in the amount of paperwork and a parallel increase in

[3] Quoted in Koenig, *The Truman Administration: Its Principles and Practices,* pp. 122, 125.

[4] Wohlstetter, *Pearl Harbor: Warning and Decision,* pp. viii–ix, 397–401.

the personnel needed to analyze the tremendous influx of information into the system. The growing numbers of decisions which must be made quickly has generated a search not only for more efficient and more coordinated information-gathering procedures, but also a search for a more favorable balance between centralized and decentralized decision-making patterns.[5]

With the rise of new states and closed societies in the postwar world has come the need to deal with people as well as with their governments. More attention has had to be paid to the many forces, factions, and interests that exist within the domestic political systems of these states. Consequently, an intensified effort has been made to discover more productive educational, cultural, and propaganda procedures. The use of these new communicative and propagandistic tools has grown to major importance in projecting a favorable image of the United States. In addition, with the forceful advent of these new instruments has arisen the need to coordinate more closely a nation's actions with its words. Thus, such problems as "managed news," open diplomacy, and imagery projection have become essential elements in the foreign-policy process, and they have had to be integrated into the policy formulation and execution phases of the process to achieve payoff value.

The recent widespread appearance of international and regional groupings—the United Nations, defense and other alliances, and economic unions, for instance—has led to a "new

[5] There appears to be little disagreement among political scientists that these communications and technological improvements have produced great problems for the American foreign-policy process. However, there are vastly differing interpretations on what trends these improvements have produced within the policy-making process. For example, Sorauf believes that the decision-making process is becoming more and more dispersed, while Brzezinski and Huntington, in *Political Power: USA/USSR*, p. 433, believe that the modern world is pushing a greater concentration of decision-making into fewer and fewer hands.

diplomacy" that challenges such traditional diplomatic methods as secret diplomacy and bilateral negotiations. In the "new diplomacy," negotiations are conducted in a continuous sustained fashion never before attempted by American statesmen, and also under the klieg lights of world opinion.

The interacting transformations analyzed above have had a tremendous impact on both the external and internal dimensions of the American foreign-policy process. Just as the traditional international boundaries between foreign and domestic affairs, peace and war, and public and private concerns have become vague, so have the boundaries blurred within the American foreign-policy process itself—between legislative and executive affairs, civilian and military concerns, and policy formulation and execution. The result is a fluid and complicated environment in which to formulate foreign policy. Acute frustrations and satisfactory compromises have alternated in the search to improve both the machinery and the personnel within the policy process.

The Secretary of State in his role of policy maker has faced both obstacles and opportunities in his efforts to adjust the American foreign-policy machine to the new and changing features of the international relations environment. To demonstrate the fundamental changes in interrelationships that have occurred, and to highlight their effects on the role of the Secretary of State, an analysis will be undertaken of seven major problem areas within the American foreign-policy process since World War II. These overlapping and mutually related areas include: (1) the heightened importance of both Congress and public opinion in the foreign-policy process; (2) the increased tensions of civil–military relations; (3) institutional proliferation; (4) the growth of the "Presidency"; (5) problems within the Department of State; (6) the changing nature of diplomacy; and (7) the dilemmas of the office of the Secretary of State itself.

The profound intrusion of the problems of foreign affairs on the lives of the American people, coupled with the uncertainty inherent in the solving of problems in the "external realm," have created difficult situations for foreign-policy makers in their relations both with the public and with Congress. For in this transformed world environment, foreign policy, instead of remaining the province of a few professionals, has become a part of everyday life for the American people. In these times of rapid communications and revolutionary upheavals, the state of the world has become a personal question for each individual.

Immediately after the war most Americans were not ready, or willing, to accept the new demands that were placed on them and on American resources. Many violently denounced their foreign-policy makers, and especially the Secretary of State, who soon became the official scapegoat for Americans who resented the sacrifices of two world wars and the frustration of their idealistic hopes for permanent peace. The Truman Administration's inability to establish an absolute formula for peace in Korea exacerbated those feelings of disillusionment. Many Americans had not foreseen the difficulties that precluded final solutions inherent in the problems of the international arena. In fact, in 1946, Dean Acheson warned both the American people and American statesmen that they must change their perceptions on the nature of international problems:

> . . . it [involvement in foreign affairs] is a long and tough job and one for which we as a people are not particularly suited. We believe that any problem can be solved with a little ingenuity and without inconvenience to the folks at large. We have trouble-shooters to do this. And our name for problems is significant. We call them headaches. You take a powder and they are gone. These pains about which we have been talking are not like that. They are like the pain of earning a living. They will stay with us until death.[6]

[6] Acheson, "Random Harvest: The Perverted Ingenuity of Propaganda," p. 635.

The American public has had to be educated to the burdens and responsibilities of sustained involvement in foreign affairs. Since the public's relations to our foreign affairs is a major, perhaps the major, factor in our diplomacy, the Secretary of State has had to cultivate an understanding of foreign relations within the American electorate. In effect, the Secretary of State must give style and cohesion to American foreign policy, while at the same time he educates the American public to a fuller understanding of the nature of United States foreign-policy commitments.

Since World War II, the President and his Secretaries of State have found that they cannot shoulder their foreign-affairs task without the constant support of Congress. Congress, in turn, has found that most of its legislative acts affect some aspect of foreign policy. Since foreign and domestic policies are two sides of the same coin, the separation-of-powers concept has been greatly altered—the President has become an important legislator, while Congress, through its control of the purse strings and its increased investigating activities, has grown in executive functions. The result has been a quantitative increase in the Secretary of State's interactions with Congress. The Secretary must testify before numerous congressional committees, inform key Congressmen and Senators of policy innovations in special private sessions, and improve liaison techniques between Congress and the Department of State. He has, in short, become the pivotal figure in cultivating the congressional consensus needed to carry out the foreign-policy program of a democratic state.

It is also with the Congress that the Secretary of State and the State Department have had their most violent confrontations, for both historical and political reasons: 1) the Department, unlike most other agencies of the government, has no special interest groups to advance its policies; 2) members of Congress generally view the State Department as being snobbish, high-handed, undemocratic, and alienated, given to involving the country unnecessarily in affairs abroad; 3) Congress often suspects the State Department of championing the causes of foreigners at the expense of the national interests; 4) the Secretary of State is the personification of international difficulties and frustration to many Congressmen, who often attack him, in addition, as an indirect way of hitting at the President; 5) the Secretary of State and the Department of State can be criticized by a member of Congress without much danger of losing votes in his local bailiwick; 7) Congress complains that the Department is obstructive to the democratic process when it at times withholds certain information from legislators.[7]

The most dramatic confrontation between Congress and the State Department was Senator Joseph McCarthy's Communist witchhunt during the early 1950's. The initial shock was devastating, as Americans lost confidence in both the State Department and the Truman Administration. Worse, the effects were not temporary; McCarthyism produced at least two continuing obstacles to proficient policy making within the State Department. First, reporting by Foreign Service officers became, and is still, less critical and more timid in its recommendations. And, second, a feeling among State Department personnel was firmly entrenched that responsibility should be spread as widely as possible on important issues so that no one person could be blamed for a policy failure at a later date. Other problems, such as good people leaving the Department and the assignment of the wrong people to the wrong positions, even fifteen years later, can be traced to the effects of McCarthyism.

[7] These points can be found elaborated upon in the following sources: Graebner, *An Uncertain Tradition: American Secretaries of State in the Twentieth Century,* p. vi; DeConde, *The American Secretary of State,* p. 145; Rosenau, "The Senate and Dean Acheson: A Case Study in Legislative Attitudes," pp. 353, 811; "Misunderstood Men," *Harper's,* p. 18.

Samuel P. Huntington, in *The Common Defense* (New York: Columbia University Press, 1961, p. 426), has written:

The drastic changes in the external environment following World War II made national security policy the overriding goal of the nation's foreign policy . . . . Security was no longer the gift of nature —the starting point of policy. Instead, it now had to be the product of conscious and sustained effort—the end result of policy. It became the dominant goal of foreign policy, with foreign policy itself often defined as a branch of national security policy.

Indeed, with the increasing importance of nuclear weapons and military strength in the mutual deterrence balance between the United States and the Soviet Union, the President and the Secretary of State have given extensive attention to strategic policies and military requirements. An adequate framework for strategic policy is no longer limited to military considerations; it must embrace the whole range of interlocked purposes and instruments involved in the foreign-policy process. For the military strength that has succeeded in deterring aggression has merely bought time and opportunity to readjust military strategy and tactics to the changing nature of modern warfare, as major power conflicts have been replaced by indirect aggression, limited warfare, and "wars of liberation." The confluence of the war and peace variables within the postwar environment has magnified the need to integrate military and nonmilitary instruments within the foreign-policy process.

With the advent of defense alliances, military-aid missions, and guerrilla warfare, the old division between "political" and "military" has virtually disappeared. Military force levels and weapons systems have become indispensable factors in the diplomatic equations of the international arena. There is increasing need that the machinery for the integration of civilian and military viewpoints operate smoothly and responsibly, so that the President and his Secretary of State can control military means for the larger political ends. Accordingly, the continuing appraisal of political-military relationships has become an essential function of the Secretary of State. The Secretary of State, with the President's assistance, must give the highest priorities to smooth relations with the Secretary of Defense and to open relations at higher levels between the Defense Department and the State Department.

The Secretary of State sets the style for cooperation between the military and civilians within those inescapable interconnections existing in policy issues such as disarmament, nuclear testing, and resource allocations. Wise Presidential selection and use of the Secretary of State in the policy process is an indespensable factor in maintaining the proper balance and mixture of the military inputs with the other requirements of foreign policy.

The emergence of the United States as one of two superpowers in the post-World War II environment has resulted in a proliferation of governmental and economic agencies interested in policy making and its implementation, and has forced significant readjustments upon the foreign-policy mechanism. A United States Senate document on foreign commerce, published in 1960, reported:

> The State Department's ability to coordinate foreign economic policy has declined greatly because of fragmentation, institutional proliferation, differing concepts of goals of economic policy, and a lack of Department of State economic experts.[8]

Dean G. Pruitt in his study, *Problem Solving in the Department of State* (Denver, Colorado: University of Denver, 1965,

[8] U.S. Senate, 86th Congress, 2nd Session, *The Role of the State Department in Coordinating the Reciprocal Trade Agreements Program,* pp. 2–4, 43–44 (paraphrased).

p. 37), interviewed a participant in the foreign-policy process, and elaborated as follows:

He [the respondent] told us that three agencies connected with internal affairs, the Departments of Interior, Commerce, and Agriculture, always support one another in conflicts against the Department of State. . . .

And former Secretary of Defense Robert A. Lovett, testifying before the Senate Subcommittee on National Security Machinery on February 23, 1960, clarified what he identified as the "foul-up factor" in the foreign-policy process:

Whether or not this itch to get in the act is a form of status seeking, the idea seems to have got around that just because some decision may affect your activities, you automatically have a right to take part in making it. . . .

The interlocking of the military, political, and economic aspects of foreign policy has resulted in a rash of interdepartmental committees, burgeoning importance of the Defense Department, and the establishment of task forces, study groups, and country teams. Simultaneously, the "noise" and "static" within the foreign-policy process has grown in quality and quantity, a situation that has made the coordinating task of the Secretary of State and his department extremely complicated.

These changes and innovations in the foreign-policy process have both increased and decreased the role of the Secretary of State. On the one hand, since the Secretary and the State Department must rely on other departments and agencies for support in most of their undertakings, the Secretary must coordinate all the pieces of policy recommendations elicited from these various sources into a comprehensive strategic framework. On the other hand, the multiplication of departments, agencies, and committees interested in the making of foreign policy has tended to force more and more of the burden for decisions upward to the Presidency itself. Many times the President seems the only one who can define where departmental lines of decision and action integratively converge. In addition, the responsibility for nuclear decisions lies directly with the President. For these reasons, the President rarely can turn to only one man or one department for advice and assistance on a major matter.

For the Secretary of State in his traditional role as primary adviser and confidant to the President on matters of foreign policy, this has created three major challenges:

1. As the office of the Presidency has grown in size and importance, Presidential assistants, special advisers, and *ad hoc* Presidential crisis groups have come to prominence, many times at the expense of the Secretary of State in his role as chief foreign-policy coordinator. Specific examples of these types of instrusions into the President–Secretary of State relationship include: (1) McGeorge Bundy as Special Assistant for National Security Affairs under Presidents Kennedy and Johnson; (2) the *ad hoc* committee that President Kennedy convened to draft alternative policy suggestions before the showdown in the Cuban Missile Crisis; and (3) the Clay Committee report on Foreign Aid made public in 1963. Not only is it possible for conditions and circumstances almost to exclude the influence of the Secretary in key decisions, more importantly the growing number of staff advisers within the office of the President causes disruptions in the personal relationship which must be the foundation of a productive President–Secretary of State partnership.

2. As President Truman said in January, 1946:

> The spectacular progress of science in recent years . . . has speeded internal development and has changed world relationships so fast that we must realize the fact of a new era. It is an era in which affairs have become complex and rich in promise. Delicate and intricate relationships, involving us all in countless ways, must be carefully considered.

To deal with these specialized scientific and technical problem areas, the President over the last decade has constructed a web of special interdepartmental committess, advisory groups, and task forces. And even when the Secretary of State attends, or is represented at, these meetings, they still raise an additional organizational barrier between the President and his Secretary of State and the State Department. Filtered through committees, the Secretary's voice becomes muted, his words blurred. His responsibilities to the President remain, but his power and authority to exercise them diminish.

Introduction of new computer techniques and data analysis has required the lateral entry of technical specialists into the higher levels of the policy process, leaving Foreign Service officers trained in the generalist tradition frustrated and disgruntled. The resulting friction between the specialists and the Foreign Service officers has undermined the quality of advice the Secretary of State is able to give in key technological areas. Until all the personnel in the Department accepts the more specialized economic and scientific techniques, the Secretary cannot efficiently integrate United States scientific activities into the larger framework of American foreign policy. As Adolph Berle has said, in advocating more scientific diplomatic procedures in the modern world environment:

> Social and economic conditions, national or (to a lesser extent) international, have begun to be susceptible of a measure of control and therefore, to that extent, have become a matter of choice. From that development a changed diplomatic outlook results.[9]

3. No factors have had more effect upon the position of the

[9] Adolf A. Berle, "Diplomacy and the New Economics," *The Dimensions of Diplomacy,* Editor, E. A. J. Johnson (Baltimore, Maryland: Johns Hopkins Press, 1964), pp. 89–90. In addition, see McClelland, *Theory and the International System,* p. 136.

Secretary of State since World War II than improvement in the art of communications and the vast increase of American commitments throughout the world. Informational, cultural, foreign-aid, and similar programs, people-to-people campaigns, good-will visits, grass-roots approaches, unilateral pronouncements and gestures, news conferences, military-aid missions, and the rapid speed of world communications have had a tremendous impact on the Secretary of State's role. The Secretary has had to sell, as well as negotiate, not only in the publicity markets of the world, but also within the political policy-making process at home. At the same time that demands on the Secretary have risen, three postwar diplomatic phenomena—crisis diplomacy, open diplomacy, and summit diplomacy—have undermined his resources.

As noted above, the dominant factors of volume and speed have tended to negate the coordination of policy at the lower administrative levels. There is so much to be correlated and so little time to do it that the adverse effects of structural difficulties have been multiplied. The rapid succession of problems that have demanded action has forced the United States to operate on the treadmill of crisis diplomacy. These demands for rapid decisions have had a centralizing influence on the diplomatic process. Thus, there is a growing tendency for the President to be his own Secretary of State or to depend on special informal advisers in the White House itself to avoid the slower-moving machinery of the State Department.

The concept of open diplomacy, bolstered by the political and technological structures of the postwar international system (e.g., the United Nations), has gained widespread acceptance in the international community. Feeling among national foreign-policy makers is now general that public opinion and mass support are essential in the evolution of a diplomatic policy. So today negotiations increasingly are held in the spotlight of world publicity. Unfortunately, the usual result is that the negotiations themselves become more important to the participants than the conclusion of agreements. Propaganda victories and imagery projection are replacing the search for the common interest as the goal of diplomatic negotiations. This is often to the dismay of those Secretaries of State who are products of the traditional school of diplomacy that stresses secrecy, compromise, and confidence as the bases of international accord.

The bipolar nature of the international environment after World War II generated a belief among many Americans that all the problems between the United States and the Soviet Union could be solved if only the leaders of the two countries could sit down together and talk things over. This belief, reinforced by open diplomacy, helped to induce a marked expansion of summit diplomacy after World War II. The result, again, was to complicate the job of the Secretary of State. Summit meetings tended to lessen flexibility, create illusions, place excessive stress on personality factors, produce a "football" atmosphere, and generate a "court of last appeal" effect. Dean Rusk, long before he became Secretary of State, warned against the excessive use and/or abuse of this diplomatic technique:

> Summit diplomacy is . . . a technique to be employed rarely and under the most exceptional circumstances, with rigorous safeguards against its becoming a debilitating or dangerous habit.[10]

The office of the Secretary of State is a position of dilemmas from which no occupant of the office in the post-World War II environment can escape. The pressures and counterpressures that have been unleashed upon the Secretary of State have increased the tensions within the office itself. The Secretary must be nonpartisan so that foreign-policy issues do not become divisive and dangerous campaign issues; yet he must back the

[10] Rusk, "The President," p. 361.

President's final policy decisions with enthusiasm as he cannot alienate himself from his Chief Executive. He must satisfy Congress to insure legislative support for Administration policies; yet he must protect foreign allies, friends, and statesmen against abusive congressional attacks. He must be a policy adviser to the President; yet he cannot neglect his tasks as manager of a large department and advocate of its policy suggestions lest he lose the confidence and respect of his colleagues and subordinates. He must maintain an alliance structure based on the common interests of a coalition diplomacy; yet he must protect and espouse American national interests. He must elicit help from other departments and agencies in the construction of foreign policy; yet he must struggle to retain his primacy as the foremost adviser to the President on foreign-policy issues. One thing is quite clear: the Secretary of State faces the difficult task of achieving a delicate balance between a variety of incompatible roles.

In summary, then, the foreign-policy process of the United States, due to the interaction of the numerous factors discussed above, has changed dramatically since World War II. And at the center of the revolutionary forces that have generated this transformation stands the office of the Secretary of State. The difficulties facing the Secretary in his role as a policy maker are enormous. However, for a man who is capable of channeling the fluidity within the policy-making process long enough to give it meaning and direction, there is more than a challenge—there is an opportunity.

CHAPTER TWO

A Policy-Making Pattern: Dean Acheson as Secretary of State

The Secretaryship of Dean Acheson from 1949 to 1953 was a period of transition for American foreign policy and for the office of the Secretary of State. Much had happened in the postwar years to change the nature of foreign relations for the United States and for the world; however it was during the Acheson Secretaryship that the full dimensions of the new problems confronted the American policy-making apparatus. Dean Acheson's operating techniques and procedures resulted in a high output of personal influence in the policy-making process and an extremely high output of important foreign policies from the Truman Administration. These policies today remain fundamental pillars for the actions of the United States in the international system.

The policy-making pattern of Acheson demonstrated several important assumptions that permeate his thoughts about the role of the Secretary as a policy maker. The first is his belief that a junior–senior hierarchical relationship between the Secretary of State and his President is essential to the success of the Secretary. Acheson also contends that policies must, at times, be formulated free from excessive public intrusion into the process of policy creation—this is based on his perception of foreign-policy formulation as being the predominant duty of professionals. And finally, he believes that the executive branch of the government is charged with primacy in conducting the foreign relations of the United States. Hence, the Acheson years will be examined to discover the basic philosophical perceptions and environmental circumstances that helped determine the policy choices made by the Truman Administration. In addition, an analysis will be made of Dean Acheson's policy-making pattern and its payoff values for him.

The bipolar confrontation between the United States and the Soviet Union and the changing power relationships within the international arena were fully in motion as Acheson assumed office. However, the questions of how these phenomena were to be interpreted, how they were to be assimilated into the policy-making apparatus, and what directions American foreign policy should follow were all unresolved. The Truman Doctrine and the Marshall Plan had committed the United States to involvement in world affairs, but no permanent commitments had been made by the United States. Congress and the American people were concerned about America's increased importance in world affairs; yet it was clear that neither Congress nor the American public fully realized the magnitude of the costs involved. Adjustments had been made within the executive branch to deal with the quantitative increase of foreign relations: nevertheless, Acheson inherited many new administrative problems, both within the

Department itself and in its relationships with other policy-making units, particularly the Department of Defense.

James F. Byrnes and General George C. Marshall, President Truman's previous Secretaries of State, had served too briefly to drastically affect the policy-making patterns within the Department. When Acheson became Secretary, he was, in effect, the first full-time postwar Secretary of State; and, owing to his close identification with the President and the major policies of the Truman Administration, he became the symbol of the successes and the failures of American foreign policy under the Truman Presidency.

Nineteen forty-nine, which Eric F. Goldman calls the "year of shocks," produced three serious foreign-policy setbacks for the Truman Administration—the "fall of China," the explosion of the A-bomb by Russia, and the conviction of Alger Hiss. In addition, Acheson's statement on the Hiss case: "I do not intend to turn my back on Alger Hiss," caused numerous accusations against both Acheson and the Truman Administration concerning their handling of the "communist situation." Accordingly, these interacting events forced the Administration to launch a comprehensive reappraisal of both its foreign and military policies, while at the same time countering the charges of Senator McCarthy that it was "soft on Communism." The aggression of North Korea a year later added another conflict to the already staggering tasks of the Truman Administration: defense in Europe, determination of a long-term policy toward Germany, and revitalization of American arms production.

With the international developments of 1949 and 1950 Dean Acheson was quickly pushed into the American spotlight: the man who had been closely, though quietly, identified with American foreign policies since the end of World War II now became chief spokesman for the Truman Administration. The office of Secretary of State became a visible decisional unit to an increasing number of Americans interested in the foreign policies of the United States. Both critics and advocates of the Truman Administration served to elevate the office of the Secretary of State and the personality of Dean Acheson to a level of public recognition never before attained by a holder of that office. This new visibility has had both positive and negative effects on the role of the Secretary of State—negative in that the Secretary is often blamed for decisions and events far beyond his control, and positive in that the Secretary can use his increased recognition as a potent instrument for reinforcing his position.

Acheson not only became the symbol of the Truman Administration; he also became operationally its leading formulator of foreign-policy foundations and policy directives. Indeed, due to historical events and domestic politics, the Secretaryship of Dean Acheson emerged as a watershed of patterns, initiatives, and innovations. And even though Acheson himself has refused to separate the policies of his Secretaryship from the eight-year period of the Truman Presidency, it is a fact that his four years as Secretary of State was the period during which most major new policies were either initiated or made operational. These policies include NATO, the Point Four Program, the Military Assistance Program, the rearming of Germany, the decision to take part in the Korean conflict, and the Uniting for Peace Resolution in the United Nations. In effect, Acheson's Secretaryship was a time when flesh was put on the skeleton of containment. As Secretary Acheson stated, on February 15, 1951, while discussing American policy toward the North Atlantic Treaty area:

> We have passed through the period of organization; we have passed through the phase of planning; we have passed through a time of the awakening of people to the nature of the true danger in the world. We are now deep in the period of action.[1]

[1] Quoted in U.S. Department of State, *The Joint Defense of Western Europe,* p. 13.

When General Marshall resigned as Secretary of State and was replaced by Dean Acheson, most commentators did not anticipate any major change in policies toward the Soviet Union. However, they underestimated the strength of the new Secretary's dislike and fear of the U.S.S.R.[2] At the time of his appointment Acheson reportedly said, "The Soviet Union is the only conspiracy that became a state, yet continues to remain a conspiracy." He viewed the Soviet Union as a national power and Communism as a militant ideology which combined presented a grave threat to the United States, to the free world, and to freedom itself. Not only was the vast expansion of the Soviet military capacity exceeding any reasonable defense needs an ominous sign, but Communism as an international movement was simultaneously seeking, by subversion and penetration, to destroy the capacity and will of noncommunist nations to resist Soviet power. The combination of Russian imperialism and Communist ideology was judged by Acheson to be "... fatal to a free society and to human rights and fundamental freedoms."

Explicity, Acheson, as spokesman for the Truman Administration, described five barriers to peace that the Soviet Union raised in the postwar world: (1) the Soviet efforts to bring about

[2] McLellan, *The Cold War in Transition,* p. 18. Two points must be be made clear at this juncture: first, many of the concepts, techniques, and methods mentioned in this chapter will be analyzed more fully in the following chapters; for example, Acheson's attitude toward the United Nations and open diplomacy will be examined in greater depth in Chapter 3.

Second, since this chapter is an attempt to describe Acheson's strategic image and operating pattern while he was Secretary of State, and not an attempt to justify the "good or evil" of the policy outputs of the Truman Administration, criticisms or praise from commentators over such bitterly contested events as the "fall of China" will be mentioned only if they help to describe or explain Acheson's operational techniques. Therefore, justifications for specific policy decisions will not be discussed unless they add to a fuller explanation of how Acheson perceived his role as a policy maker.

the collapse of the non-Soviet world in order to fulfill a prediction of Soviet theory made genuine negotiations most difficult; (2) the shroud of secrecy which the Soviet leaders wrapped around the people and the states they controlled seriously deterred international communications; (3) the rate at which the Soviet Union was building armaments and armies gravely endangered world peace; (4) the use by the Soviet leaders of the international Communist movement for direct and indirect aggression produced tensions and distrust throughout the world; and (5) the Soviet use of violence to impose its will and its political system upon other people violated the right of nations to chart their own destinies.

It was upon this interpretative diagnosis of the Soviet threat that the Truman Administration formulated its firm policy of containment against the thrusts of the Soviet Union and Communism. The catchwords of the Truman-Acheson brand of containment were "situations of strength," "strength at the center," "total diplomacy," "national interest," "self-help," "the missing component," and "the prevention of war"—all of which were linked by the central belief that the United States had to provide "the spark of leadership" needed to supply material and psychological support for those nations wanting to remain free from Soviet domination.

The concept of "situations of strength" was based on Acheson's belief that the United States must be strong enough to keep the peace. Acheson was sure that the Soviet Union's influence would flow into any vacuum of power that existed around its periphery; therefore, the United States must establish military, political, and economic positions of strength wherever situations of weakness were thought to exist. Moreover, no meaningful negotiations with the Soviet Union would be possible until the free world succeeded in convincing the Soviet leaders that they could not in any way profit from a policy of expansion. When, in a television interview on September 18, 1950, Acheson was asked: "You have talked often about situations of strength. Is that a fundamental basis of American foreign policy?" Acheson replied categorically, "It is an absolutely essential and fundamental basis."

The integrated and balanced economic and military arrangements between Western Europe and the United States were another key to discouraging Soviet expansion. Secretary Acheson emphasized the need for "strength at the center" in the same television interview cited above. To Edward R. Murrow's question: "Where is our major weight to be put in this shifting contest with the Soviet Union?" Acheson replied:

> It is very hard to put our major attention anywhere. We have to look at all these points [throughout the world] and work at all of them together. But I think that we must put our major effort at the present moment into creating strong North Atlantic defense forces. If we have these forces—united, balanced, collective forces—strong, well-equipped, able and ready to deter aggression, then problems all over the world take on a different shape. Such forces alone will change problems in Greece, in Turkey, and in Yugoslavia, in the Middle East and in the Far East.

In order to establish a coalition of free states "united at the center," organization and infrastructure had to be added to the North Atlantic Treaty agreement. And Acheson was instrumental in the construction of the organization that became basic to security within the North Atlantic Treaty area. President Truman writes in his *Memoirs* (Vol II, p. 253):

> . . . Secretary Acheson worked with great patience and skill to drive home the point that NATO would have no meaning at all unless a really joint effort was made at common defense and mutual aid, and his arguments won the day. There would have been no NATO without Dean Acheson.

Two salient facts were apparent to Secretary Acheson: first, there was a necessary and even desirable interrelationship among the multifarious elements of the foreign-policy process. Second, the nature of the Soviet threat was an all-encompassing thrust at all levels of intensity and with all types of weapons. Not only was Soviet military power a challenge; poverty, disease, and ignorance were also feeding grounds for communism. To combat Soviet pressures on the psychological, economic, educational, and political levels, Western military strength was not enough. "Total diplomacy" was required to meet the total Soviet threat.

President Truman and Secretary Acheson quite frankly stressed self-interest as the basic motive for NATO, the military-assistance program, foreign aid, and other national-security policies. These programs, in Acheson's mind at least, were not part of a crusade against evil or of a worldwide humanitarian movement; they were practical necessities. Thus, on Russian steps needed to facilitate negotiations with the United States, Acheson commented, ". . . they have been formulated by us, not as moralists but as servants of government, anxious to get on with . . . practical problems . . . [free] from fear and uncertainty."[3] And, even more candidly, on the unifying bases of NATO:

> The thing that really holds the integrated force together is the continuing conviction that the national interest of each party is most effectively served by working together through the integrated force.[4]

Secretary Acheson's emphasis on "the missing component" and "self-help" stemmed from a conviction that American power and resources were limited. He was confident that the United States could provide the missing component for the newly emerging African and Asian nations—economic aid and military assistance—only if these nations were able to solidify their own internal political systems. The will and the determination required to produce viable political systems had to come from

[3] Quoted in Bundy, *The Pattern of Responsibility,* pp. 39–40.

[4] Quoted in U.S. Department of State, *The Joint Defense of Western Europe,* p. 12.

within these young states; likewise, the domestic decisions necessary for their success and stability.

"The missing component" and "self-help" guidelines also were incorporated into the Administration's operational policy toward political unification of Western Europe. Though President Truman and Secretary Acheson became increasingly interested in European unification and were willing to assist in its progress, they remained convinced that the final decision lay with the Europeans themselves.

A final premise of the Truman Administration's strategic framework for containing Soviet power was that war is not inevitable. Again and again, Truman and Acheson underscored the fact that American military strength was meant, first, to deter wars; or, failing that, to fight wars within controllable limits at the lowest possible levels of intensity. Acheson personally found the concepts of preventive war, total victory, and class warfare as inappropriate doctrines on which to formulate strategic foreign policy. Both he and Truman believed that to be truly secure the United States must preserve its freedom without recourse to another world war.

In summary, the Truman Administration's policy guidelines envisaged a strong Europe, peaceful coexistence of the United States with Russia and China, balanced military forces, and continuing leadership of the free world by the United States. By 1952 Acheson was sure that these policy patterns were succeeding in preventing Soviet aggression.[5]

[5] For example, Acheson pointed out the shift toward a less aggressive policy during the Nineteenth Congress of the Communist Party of the Soviet Union in Moscow in October, 1952. "Acheson Sees Ike's Foreign Policy as 'Bluster and Bluff,'" *U.S. News & World Report,* 41, No. 14 (October 5, 1956), p. 89. An interesting point is that Marshall D. Shulman, who was on Acheson's staff, marks the Nineteenth Congress of the C.P.S.U. as the turning point in Soviet foreign policy, also. Shulman, *Stalin's Foreign Policy Reappraised,* pp. 1–12.

The fact that Secretary Acheson was the most important formulator and coordinator of foreign-policy principles and guidelines during the Truman Administration has been disputed by neither his admirers nor his critics. A study of the operating techniques through which he assumed and retained his special role will lead, in later chapters, to consideration of more abstract and general rules in Acheson's operational code for the office of Secretary of State in the policy-making arena.

Dean Acheson, when he became Secretary of State, immediately recognized the necessity for effective communication between the Department of State and Congress, and it was under his direction that the first permanent Assistant Secretary of State for Congressional Relations was instituted. Although he knew that congressional approval of administration policies was a prerequisite to a strong and united foreign-policy program, he had no intention of compromising either his principles or his style. In Acheson's view, executive-legislative relations were never meant to be peaceful: it was the process of "power striking power" that provided the dynamism for the policy-making system. He also believed that the prospects of a Secretary of State obtaining approval of Administration policies would improve if he based his relations with Congress on mutual respect rather than on mutual friendliness. When these attitudes toward Congress encountered the passions unleashed by the "fall of China," the rise of McCarthyism, and the strains of the Korean War, Acheson's relations with Congress became difficult and sometimes bitter. Yet, with the exception of the House defeat of the Korea Aid Bill of 1949 (by a vote of 193–191), he was able to secure congressional approval for every major piece of the Truman Administration's foreign-policy program. How did he attain this high level of policy endorsement from a Congress that had little love for him personally?

Acheson's attitude toward Congress rested on four operational pillars: (1) his belief that he was a defender of the Presidential prerogative in foreign affairs, (2) his practice of discussing policy innovations and recommendations with key Congressmen and Senators on an individual and informal basis, (3) his conviction that Congress was not, and could not be, a creator in the foreign-policy process, and (4) his ability to be well-prepared when appearing before congressional committees.

Secretary Acheson strongly endorsed President Truman's desire to prevent congressional encroachments upon executive prerogatives in the area of foreign policy. As the President's spokesman and protector before congressional committees, he was able to add both prestige to his position within the executive branch and an authoritative dimension to his relations with the legislative branch.[6] On the one hand, the President was confident that Secretary Acheson would present a strong case for the executive branch in its continuing struggle with Congress, and on the other hand, Congress was sure that Secretary Acheson spoke for the President, that what he told its members was Administration policy. Thus by becoming identified as a spokesman for strong Presidential leadership in foreign affairs, Acheson increased his official stature in both the executive and legislative policy-making arenas.

Acheson's technique of relying on a few important Congressmen to push Administration foreign policies was adopted after a more encompassing approach had failed. Soon after he had assumed office, the new Secretary called together an unofficial conference of Congressmen to explain positions of the Administration and to reply to questions. This was done ostensibly to

[6] U.S. Senate, 81st Congress, 1st Session Committee on Foreign Relations, *Nomination of Dean G. Acheson,* January 13, 1949, p. 17; Acheson, *A Citizen Looks at Congress,* pp. 69–70; interview with Pat Holt, April 15, 1966; interview with John M. Vorys, April 22, 1966.

bring Congress into the making of foreign policy and to make it possible for the Secretary and Congress to meet on neutral ground—but it failed. Since Acheson himself was under fire from congressional critics, he could not remove the Secretaryship from political warfare. The Congressmen demonstrated more interest in polemical attacks on Acheson than in pursuing profound analyses of foreign-policy alternatives.

Thereafter, Secretary Acheson abandoned the procedure of trying to deal with Congress in large gatherings. Instead, he became a master at cultivating the support and trust of key members of the congressional committees whose support, he felt, was essential to the Administration. In his book A *Citizen Looks At Congress,* Acheson wrote:

> Each of these committees tends to develop a life of its own, in which members hold individual, rather than strictly party, attitudes and where the influence of strong and set characters is great. For instance, the attitude of Senator Millikin of Colorado toward reciprocal trade legislation in the Finance Committee . . . was more likely to influence than to be influenced by the views of others, including a President of [his] own party. (pp. 24–25)

Senate Committee chairmen, Senators Tom Connally and Arthur Vandenberg of the Foreign Relations Committee and Richard Russell of the Armed Services Committee, were special confidantes. In addition, recognizing the growing postwar importance of the House of Representatives in foreign policy, Acheson cultivated the support of leading members of the House Foreign Affairs Committee. Some members of Congress not included in the "inner circle" were resentful, but the limited congressional participation of a few leaders in the earlier stages of the policy-making process proved effective toward achievement of Administration goals.

Secretary Acheson was unalterably opposed to any attempt by Congress to formulate foreign-policy initiatives or innovations.

Congress was, in his view, structurally and ideologically incapable of creating a consistent, long-range foreign-policy program. He urged instead that Congress perform those functions in the foreign-policy process for which it was best prepared—approving, modifying, and vetoing of executive recommendations. Although many Congressmen accused Secretary Acheson of placing policies before them as "faits accomplis," others agreed that the proper role of Congress was to review, not create, foreign policy.

Secretary Acheson spent long hours preparing for committee hearings. At times he complained about the proliferation of committees concerned with foreign policy, but he rarely thought it a waste of time to thoroughly prepare himself for these committee hearings. Thus, John M. Vorys, a prominent Republican member of the House Foreign Affairs Committee and a critic of the Truman Administration's foreign-policy programs, nevertheless expressed deep admiration for Secretary Acheson as a committee witness because one could tell that he had "done his homework."

One of Acheson's most rewarding tactics was his stress on American self-interest and national security as the basis for the majority of the policies which he presented to Congress. Congressmen appreciated the idea of a payoff value from the money they allotted for the Administration's foreign-policy programs.

Even though Acheson sometimes got himself into difficulties with committee members by "forgetting to put a bridle on his tongue," or by being "too brilliant," he nevertheless retained the support of the responsible and powerful leadership of the key committees.[7]

Acheson saw the role of public opinion in American foreign

[7] Rosenau, "The Senate and Dean Acheson," p. 802. Rosenau found a perfect correlation in that the four "cordial" Republican Senators toward Secretary Acheson were all members of the Foreign Relations Committee.

policy as a bifurcated one. On the one hand, no Administration's policy could be effective without popular support; on the other hand, the American public had little place in the process of policy formulation or diplomatic negotiation. The Secretary was entirely convinced that foreign policy had become the province of all citizens, not just a few professionals, and that public opinion in the United States should be both educated and respected. On May 10, 1950, while speaking in London, he openly defended public discourse on American policy alternatives, even when at times it was confusing and hypercritical:

> . . . if I might hazard an opinion about my country, I should say that the dissonance flows from the very awareness that difficult decisions must be made and is a part of the process of making them.[8]

In pursuing his goal of education, Secretary Acheson talked about "public opinions" rather than "public opinion." Popular conceptions of what was the right foreign-policy position of the United States varied widely from group to group and from situation to situation. Acheson's conclusion was that the State Department must actively seek to educate interest groups outside Congress in the hope that the Administration's policy choices might then be discussed in a more reasoned and restrained manner.

To the American public and to the news media, Acheson constantly emphasized the difficulties and dangers confronting the United States in its relations with the world. He was determined that the people should not believe that the problems of foreign policy are easier than they are. He also repeatedly warned that the United States was not omnipotent. Nothing, he felt, would

[8] Acheson, "The Problem of International Organization Among Countries of Europe and the North Atlantic Area," *The Department of State Bulletin,* 22, No. 568 (May 22, 1950), p. 791.

more quickly lead to disaster than for the public to overestimate American power and demand action that was beyond the capabilities of the country.

Acheson faced a difficult task in seeking a balance between what he perceived as the need to formulate policies in secret and the need to inform the American people. As he said on the occasion of the release of the China White Paper in the summer of 1949:

> One of the very great and perplexing questions in the conduct of foreign affairs is the conflict that goes on in your mind between the harm you will do to some foreign nation in carrying out its policy by making a lot of material public, and the great harm that happens if the people of the United States do not understand the facts of the situation.[9]

In spite of his commitment to the principle of enlightened public opinion, Acheson could not, in the final analysis, envisage a place for the public in the formulating or negotiating stages of making policy: he remained dedicated to the traditional methods of privacy in both policy making and diplomacy. "It was the duty of the Secretary of State," he said to James Reston of *The New York Times*, "to inaugurate new policies free from public scrutiny and pressure. It was the Secretary's task to shield evolving concepts from the public." Acheson preferred to stand alone, to let the records of himself as policy formulator and of the Truman Administration's foreign-policy programs speak for themselves. The President, he believed, should be the leader in the determination of policy; the role of the public, like that of Congress, should generally be restricted to that of critic or advocate of the policy programs that the Government presented it.

One of Secretary Acheson's great strengths in formulating and

[9] Quoted in Bundy, *The Pattern of Responsibility*, p. 182.

coordinating foreign policy was the confidence that the Western Allies placed in him. Acheson's devotion to Europe was well-recognized both abroad and by President Truman. His harmonious working relations with Foreign Secretary Ernest Bevin of Great Britain, Foreign Minister Robert Schuman of France, and Chancellor Konrad Adenauer of Germany resulted in their support or, at least, acceptance of most American policies. Acheson's efforts to keep the Korean War from escalating, his concern to keep NATO a defensive alliance, and his practice of consulting the Europeans, within the context of coalition diplomacy, all met with European approval which further expanded his power base within the international policy-making arena. And on the national scene, his firm defense of American national interests when meeting with European statesmen reinforced his position as President Truman's primary adviser in the foreign-policy process. Thus Acheson's personal and intellectual attributes not only contributed to his success in diplomatic encounters with the Western Allies, but also solidified his policy-making effectiveness at both the national and international levels of the political process.

Acheson was almost alone among the postwar Secretaries of State in giving extensive attention to military strategy and to balancing the military instrument with other instruments of the foreign-policy process. Not only did he draw up an overarching strategic framework for the Truman Administration, but he also initiated a number of specific politico-military policies: he shouldered the initial responsibility for devising a formula for the conventional build-up within NATO; he was instrumental in operationalizing NSC #68, the theoretical foundation for rearming the United States when the Korean conflict erupted; and he was the foremost spokesman for the Administration's brand of deterrence based on balanced forces, limited warfare, and collective security. As a result of these strategic policies, the United States and the Western Alliance were granted a little time in which their statesmen could "consider the employment of force without having always to step at the outset into the nuclear abyss."[10] In essence, Acheson saw the need to coordinate foreign policy and military policy within a broad strategic framework based on national security and self-preservation.

It appeared obvious to Acheson that in the twentieth century the Defense and State Departments were dealing merely with different aspects of foreign policy. Therefore, he consulted with both the Joint Chiefs of Staff and the Defense Department on all important matters. The interim when Louis Johnson was Secretary of Defense saw major problems in communication, but even then Acheson was able to maintain some liaison with the Defense Department through secret meetings and personal friendships. When General Marshall returned to government as Defense Secretary, Acheson was able to restore the earlier close collaboration which he felt was invaluable to the credence of his larger strategic formulations.

Even the stresses of the Korean War did not alter Acheson's position of strategic coordinator; cooperation between the two Departments continued at all levels. Secretary Marshall describes the operating techniques:

> We had a great many discussions. It has been a rather common procedure for the Secretary of State and one or two of his principal men, Mr. Lovett [Under Secretary of Defense] and myself and the Chiefs of Staff to meet in the Chiefs of Staff room and hold discussions of two and three hours over these various matters, generally with some specific document. . . . Then we would investigate it, or the Chiefs of Staff had, through their lower working levels, and then

[10] Kaufmann, *The McNamara Strategy,* p. 106. Acheson was against any strategic policy that placed total reliance upon nuclear weapons. As a statesman, he wanted flexibility and control built into a military strategy so that he and other statesmen would not be faced with "either/or" types of situations in which compromise was impossible.

their reply had gone back informally [to State] and then this meeting would occur . . . .
We always reached agreement, and it was an agreement where the Chiefs of Staff sat on one side of the table, and Secretary of State Acheson, with his people, and Lovett and myself sat on the other; in other words, the civilians discussing it from our point of view, as nearly as I was civilian, and the military across from us . . . . Now those [policy agreements] were carried either to the Security Council or direct to the President . . . .[11]

Acheson's relations with the military benefited from his long service in the Treasury and State Departments. He was regarded as a fellow professional who merited the respect of military officers. The resulting mutual cordiality survived Acheson's reassertion of formal civilian supremacy over all phases of American foreign policy and, more particularly, his designation of the State Department as the leading policy formulator. Dean Acheson's capacity to work closely and smoothly with the military people (the "total victory" group excluded) gained him the support of the Department of Defense and the Chiefs of Staff for his important military strategic recommendations—the development of NATO strength; the rearming of Germany; the limited-warfare strategy in Korea; the refusal to accept Nationalist Chinese troops to fight in Korea; and the firing of General MacArthur.

Alexander DeConde has reported that "the decisive reason for Dean Acheson's selection [as Secretary of State] was his thorough knowledge of State Department organization and broad experience in shaping foreign policy."[12] When Acheson assumed

[11] Quoted in Millis, Mansfield, and Stein, *Arms and the State,* pp. 301–303.

[12] DeConde, *The American Secretary of State,* pp. 47, 63–64. DeConde believes that the Acheson appointment set a precedent in that there is now more weight given to professional qualifications than to political considerations in the postwar choices of men to serve as Secretaries of State.

control of the State Department, he already had both experience and knowledge in the making of foreign policy. He had served as both Under Secretary of State and Assistant Secretary of State. And as Under Secretary to General Marshall, he literally ran the department and was Marshall's Chief of Staff on all policy matters. No difficulty confronted him in communicating with the other professionals, i.e., the Foreign Service officers, within the Department of State. And his background in both the Treasury and State Departments instilled in him a particular set of decision-making procedures that he followed assiduously when he became Secretary of State.

As department head, Secretary Acheson instituted a reorganization of the State Department, especially strengthening the immediate staff of the Secretary's office; he delegated organizational and administrative authority to the Under Secretary, James Webb, to free more of his own time for policy making; he improved the institutional liaisons between the State Department and Congress; and he fostered a more harmonious relationship between the President and the Foreign Service officers by having them meet each other in small groups where is was possible to discuss foreign-policy problems. As part of his dedication to establish the State Department as the chief architect of foreign-policy alternatives, he appointed and retained advisers of the highest possible quality in the Policy Planning Staff, which was assigned one of the most difficult problems of foreign policy in a revolutionary age—striking a balance between immediate problems and future objectives.

During the McCarthy era, Acheson tried to protect his personnel from the invectives of the Wisconsin Senator, and even though Acheson himself has denigrated his effort to protect his subordinates as inadequate, he nevertheless was outspoken enough to gain the respect and loyalty of the State Department staff. One of his endeavors to dispell the damaging charges of

Senator McCarthy was reported in *The New Republic* of May 1, 1950 (Vol. 122, No. 18, p. 6):

> For 40 minutes after completing his scheduled speech, Acheson held 300 of the nation's leading editors spellbound as he tore into his enemies. Senator Joseph McCarthy sat motionless in the audience while the Secretary angrily denounced the "vicious madness" of those who have pictured the State Department as Communist-infested.

As the chief policy maker within the State Department, he was intellectually on top of his job, and he did his homework. James Reston has reported that whenever Acheson chaired a meeting on any subject, he was mentally at the head of the table. Officers, too, no longer came into meetings half-prepared or prepared only on that particular aspect of the problem in which they happened to be interested. Acheson remained in control of the Department's internal policy-making process through five fundamental operating techniques: (1) becoming a participant in the policy formulation process at the earliest possible levels; (2) listening patiently and silently to the conflicting views of his subordinates at staff meetings; (3) giving credit and rewards to those subordinates who did excellent jobs while showing little tolerance for those who were mediocre; (4) backing his subordinates completely when they had to deal with other departments; and (5) fighting hard to see that the State Department won policy battles with other departments. Thus Acheson was able to keep the policy variables within his department coordinated, active, and imaginative.

In the area of diplomacy, Secretary Acheson was quite frankly opposed to summit diplomacy, excessive Foreign Ministers' meetings, and open diplomacy. Instead he favored diplomatic procedures that permitted both the President and the Secretary of

State to stay in Washington and that were based on the traditional concept of secret diplomacy.

Acheson spent more time in Washington and less overseas than any other postwar Secretary of State. And he was extremely reluctant to see the President leave Washington to conduct actual negotiations with other nations. Acheson regarded Foreign Ministers' meetings and summit meetings as too often developing into battlegrounds for individual champions to display their particularly bright syntax and clever diplomatic maneuvers. Acheson made every effort to avoid these international encounters by arguing that it was not individual personalities that made the difference in negotiations, but rather strength and preparedness. American interests, he felt, could best be achieved through a protracted period of negotiations making full use of ambassadors, trained personnel, written communiques, and other traditional diplomatic techniques. Foreign Ministers' meetings should be held only on the most pressing problems, and only on the basis of an agreed-upon agenda. Acheson was even more cool to proposals for general, unstructured negotiations between heads of state and Foreign Ministers, since he felt such efforts raised false hopes among some people and fears among others. By the appointment of an ambassador-at-large, by the use of the traditional methods of diplomacy, by limiting negotiations to only specific subjects, and by retaining the full confidence of the Western Allies, Acheson was able to spare himself and President Truman many of the pitfalls of personal statesmanship.

From the outset of his Secretaryship, Acheson was determined not to seek compromise for its own sake or to negotiate simply to be negotiating. He placed little faith in the ability of talk sessions to produce a durable relationship with the Russians. Not only were the Russians waging a determined propaganda battle even while negotiating, but at the time of his Secretaryship Acheson was convinced that the international environment was too fluid for effective settlements. In order to reach a stable base from which to negotiate, the Western Allies must first become strong enough at the center to demonstrate to the Russians that a policy of expansion would be futile. Acheson stated his formula for fruitful negotiations:

> When we have reached unity and determination on the part of free nations—when we have eliminated all the areas of weakness that we can—we will be able to evolve working agreements with the Russians. . . .
>
> The Soviet leaders are realists. . . . As we succeed in building the necessary economic and defensive military strength, it will become clear to them that the non-Soviet world will neither collapse nor be dismembered piecemeal. Some modification in their aggressive policies may follow, if they then recognize that the best interests of the Soviet Union require a cooperative relationship with the outside world.[13]

To Acheson, negotiations would never lead to a final solution of problems between the Russians and the Americans, but, at the same time, Acheson was convinced that careful negotiations from a basis of strength would result in the Russians becoming more nation-state oriented and less ideologically motivated.

Acheson was an outspoken opponent of the postwar drift toward open diplomacy. Time and again he sought to conduct diplomatic negotiations free from the klieg lights of the news media and public opinion. He refused to conduct negotiations based on what he considered false illusions or propagandistic slogans. To Acheson, negotiations were useful only when they registered facts and were directed toward a problem that actually existed. To conduct diplomacy in the fashion of a public debate was to denigrate the effectiveness of the traditional methods of diplomacy; whether with opponents or friends, secret diplomacy was essential for satisfactory understanding. On the conclusion

[13] Quoted in Bundy, *The Pattern of Responsibility,* pp. 32–33.

of negotiations that led to the Berlin agreements in the spring of 1949, he said:

. . . agreement with the Kremlin was reached and simultaneous announcements prepared so swiftly and secretly as to avoid the leaks, contradictory explanations, and embarrassing predictions which so often confuse joint action by democratic allies.[14]

Thus, during his Secretaryship, Acheson kept to a minimum negotiations that revolved around the press, the United Nations, or heads of government. In this way, he was able to increase his bargaining power and flexibility both in the international diplomatic arena, where he was the primary Western spokesman through whom all diplomatic initiatives had to be cleared, and in the internal policy-making process, where he was chief coordinator of the traditional diplomatic channels.

Secretary Acheson's success in nurturing a "special relationship" of trust and loyalty with President Truman was the undergirding to all his power and influence, formally and informally, within the policy-making process.[15] By his capacity to gain the confidence of Truman, he was able to formulate and coordinate policy at the highest level in the most comprehensive manner. An examination will be made of four major techniques he employed to insure President Truman's confidence:

First, Acheson fully informed the President on all matters of foreign policy. He briefed the President thoroughly, approximately four times a week when he was in Washington—and he briefed him alone. When Acheson left Washington for confer-

[14] Acheson, *Sketches from Life of Men I Have Known,* p. 6.

[15] This conclusion is based on DeConde's thesis, which is that a Secretary of State can only be as effective and important as a President allows him to be. In addition, Acheson himself agrees with this interpretation: Acheson, "The President and the Secretary of State": *The Secretary of State,* pp. 27–50.

ences, he would send the President a daily cable with a full summary of the day's events. Each cable was a personal account, dictated by the Secretary himself and intended for the President alone. President Truman in his *Memoirs* (Vol. II, p. 253) reported that "Acheson always kept me fully informed about every move he intended to make."

Second, Acheson was specific about the nature of the President–Secretary of State relationship. Since he had been in the State Department for years and had seen the trouble caused by President Truman's perception of Secretary Byrnes' assumption of excessive authority in relation to the Presidential office and as he was conscious of Truman's extreme sensitivity to any encroachments on what he considered the responsibilities of the Presidency, Acheson made it crystal clear to Truman that he had no illusions of being either the President or his Prime Minister. Rather, he went out of his way to demonstrate that he fully understood that the President, and only the President, was responsible for the determination of final policy decisions.

Third, Secretary Acheson was a loyal supporter of President Truman on the personal level and in the political arena, as well as in the policy process. After the Congressional defeats of the 1946 elections, his loyalty did not waver. He supported Truman wholeheartedly in the Presidential campaign of 1948. And Acheson showed his disdain for those policy makers who tried to undercut the President either in the political arena (e.g., James Forrestal) or in the policy process (e.g., Louis Johnson). Acheson and the President worked in an atmosphere of mutual respect and trust.

Fourth, Acheson's style of decision-making blended harmoniously with President Truman's. Both preferred to make crisis decisions in small groups; both viewed the Department of State as the coordinator of foreign-policy alternatives; and both sought to avoid rigid institutionalization of the policy process. Secretary

Acheson was able to parlay these similar operating likes and dislikes into a smooth decision-making relationship.

Secretary Acheson's ability to work harmoniously with President Truman had decisive utility for him as a policy maker: In addition to participating in all the major foreign-policy decisions of the Administration, he was also the spokesman through which all major policy alternatives were presented to the President. In fact, his policy presentations were, on occasion, instrumental in effecting changes in President Truman's initial choices, for instance, in the change of attitude by the President when he finally rejected the offer of Nationalist Chinese troops to fight in Korea.

In conclusion, it can be stated that though many criticized Acheson, few doubted his authority to speak for the Administration. He, and no one else, was the President's final spokesman on foreign policy. In addition, his personal rapport with President Truman and their convergent policy-making patterns established Acheson as the primary initiator and executor of all the major foreign policies of the Truman Administration.

CHAPTER THREE

Acheson's Perceptions of International Relations

Dean Acheson's perceptions of international relations, which underlay the policies he initiated and supported during his tenure in office, have not changed through the years. An examination of Acheson's view of the international arena and the role of the United States in it will clarify the nation-state interaction aspects of the Acheson operational code.

At the center of Acheson's perception of international relations stands the phenomenon of struggle. Relations between states are never static; there is movement at all times. Each international movement, even when it ostensibly is limited to only two countries, in fact affects all. There can be no isolation in a world of ceaseless power shifts, transformed environments, and international tensions. In Acheson's words, nation states are

> bound together in a form of restless life in which forces are constantly moving, changing, in search of balanced and maintained pressure . . . the relations of nation-states are not episodic and isolated; they are continuous and inter-related.[1]

By the same token, the constant movement in international relations eliminates the possibility of utopian solutions. There are no shortcuts, no sudden dramatic gestures that will solve all international problems. Struggle between nations both in times of war and in times of peace has characterized the past and will continue to characterize the future. The elements of force, power, conflict, and war are "real" facts of international relations; they cannot be wished away or moralized away. Even the effects of military victory are transitory:

> A common and specious maxim is that what our soldiers win on the battlefield our diplomats lose at the conference table. This assumes that what is won by force is solid and lasting, that it will remain unless lost by mismanagement. Nothing could be more false. What is won by force is as transient as the colors of the sunset. Force, at most, destroys opposing force and leaves the loser defenseless. At once, almost within the hour, a wholly new situation arises.[2]

In the perpetual struggle among nations, there is a never-ending effort to maintain an equilibrium of tolerance to see that no one nation-state becomes so powerful that it can impress its particular way of life upon the other nation-states. This struggle continues in times of open conflict, cold-war tensions, and even in times of peace.

But by hard work, diplomatic skills, and man's creative intelligence, violent eruptions may be avoided. Although absolute or

[1] Acheson, *A Democrat Looks at His Party,* pp. 88–89.

[2] Acheson, *Sketches from Life of Men I Have Known,* pp. 173–174.

permanent agreements in the international system, whether in the form of alliances or supranational institutions, are doomed to failure, there still remains an area of maneuverability. The foreign policy of a state—especially one of the more powerful states—can be evaluated by how it affects and is able to control the results of the pushes and counterpushes in the international arena. Thus Acheson, a self-styled realist,[3] made policy, and continues to make policy recommendations, in the context of a worldwide struggle syndrome. An analysis of the various facets of this larger struggle framework will now be undertaken.

First is Acheson's belief in the continued existence of the nation-state as the primary actor in the international arena. National self-interest, as interpreted by official government policy makers, must be the basis for the settlement of disputes or tensions between any two states or group of states. Acheson rejects ideas of a world controlled by a supranational world government; and, more specifically, he rejects the United Nations as the locus for settlement of interstate struggles. The United Nations is no "hallowed symbol," no substitute for difficult national decisions. It is no more than the nation-states that are its members. It is reported that when Acheson was asked whether he would have preferred being U.S. Ambassador to the United Nations to being Secretary of State, he tartly replied that if he had only the first of these options, "like Seneca I would have retired to my bath and opened my veins."[4] Since there is no world community, man only deceives himself when he talks about world

[3] *Realist,* in Acheson's view, appears to mean one who is preoccupied with things and actions rather than with words. One who has the disposition to think and act in the light of things and situations as they are, or as one thinks they are, based on intelligent observations and insights, and to repudiate unrealizable or visionary schemes which are based on wishes or slogans.

[4] Quoted in Seabury, "The Establishment Game: Nicholas Murray Butler Rides Again," p. 26.

peace through world law. In criticizing the Eisenhower Administration's overreliance upon the United Nations in 1957, Acheson said:

> It will not do to say that the United Nations will determine policy, make decisions, and enforce them. The United Nations is not a supranational entity with a mind, a will, and power. It is a forum, and no more than the nations which meet there. Nothing more comes out of it than is put into it. . . .
>
> If a great nation, like the United States, looks to the United Nations to form American policy, instead of fighting in the United Nations for what the American Government believes should be done, then we have committed an unprecedented abdication of responsibility and power. . . .[5]

Second, Acheson stresses the necessity to view the world free from illusions. The American people and American statesmen need to adjust their minds to the real world; whatever their predilections, their hopes and dreams, they must recognize that

> . . . the first duty of a society is to survive. It isn't to make the world safe for democracy, or to bring about the Kingdom of Heaven on earth. It is to survive. That's the No. 1 necessity.[6]

This means first attention to immediate situations. Longer-range objectives need not be abandoned, but it is necessary here and now "to wage peace vigorously and relentlessly" so that all nations can live and hopefully prosper in their own ways. Difficult problems must be faced as they arise and are not to be avoided through the use of illusions or slogans.

In order to insure the viability of liberty and freedom in the world, American foreign-policy makers must understand the true nature, dimensions, and immediacy of the problems that confront

[5] Acheson, "Middle East Policy," *Vital Speeches,* 23, No. 8 (February 1, 1957), p. 236.

[6] Acheson, "Danger in the World—and What to Do About It," p. 119.

the United States from abroad. Only by adopting the short-range measures needed to meet the immediate challenges of today can American policy makers protect such hard-won values as freedom and liberty. For in Acheson's conceptual framework, there are no absolutes or sure things in the vast, complex realms of foreign affairs or human relations:

Some, encouraged by eminent philosophers have thought that liberty was the natural state of man and that its universal growth and acceptance was inevitable. I do not believe that for a minute. It seems to me that liberty has come to those whose stout hearts and hard heads have won it.[7]

Third, Acheson rejects the absolutist ethical approach—by which Acheson means one that attempts to apply the maxims or ideology of moral teaching to relations among states—as a legitimate guideline for conducting affairs in the complex international sphere. Too many commentators, according to Acheson, attempt to tie individual morality or a nation-state's moral system to the relations between states. The usual outcome is to pervert morality into cure-all slogans, missions, or crusades. Accordingly, those who become engrossed with a moralistic approach to international relations remain oblivious to the perils permeating the world scene, of the lightning speed with which relative positions can change, and of the pressures that emotional popular attitudes can exert toward forcing governments to foolish action or restraining them from wise action.

Morality in domestic affairs is an entirely different concept from any attempt at constructing an international moral system. Man simply cannot transpose moral parameters from the domestic to the international system:

Morality is a very slippery word in international affairs. . . .
Morality in domestic affairs is something one can understand because

[7] Acheson, "Foreign Policy Tradition of the United States," p. 551.

there one is living under a system which has enforcement agencies and agencies for formulating doctrines and enforcing doctrines. In the world, it may be that that does not exist. . . .
You are dealing with people, one half of whom deny the very foundations of what you call morality. . . .[8]

Acheson is convinced that a good deal of trouble arises in international relations because of "the anthropomorphic urge" to regard nations as individuals, and the parallel temptation to apply precepts for individual conduct to the conduct of nation-states:

The fact is that nations are not individuals; the cause and effect of of their actions are not individuals; the cause and effect of their actions are wholly different; and what a government can and should do with resources which it takes from its citizens must be governed by wholly different considerations from those which properly determine an individual's use of his own. . . .
This does not mean that considerations of compassion have no place in governmental decisions. It does mean that the criteria are generally quite different and far more complicated. . . .[9]

Acheson also rejects the "moralistic-ideological approach" to the conduct of foreign affairs because it threatens to identify in one theme both a central all-pervasive evil and the prescription for its eradication. Complexity and contradiction permeate the international scene; Acheson, therefore, insists that principles in international relations be stated in terms of their purpose and effect, not related to moral tenets, and conducted by consistent and orderly methods that promote trust and confidence in diplomacy. In this way, official policy makers may possess the flexibility needed to cope with the intricacies of international relations.

[8] Acheson, "I Don't Share the Sense of Panic," pp. 129–130.

[9] Acheson, "Ethics in International Relations Today," p. 227; Bundy, *The Pattern of Responsibility*, p. 34. Acheson does not want to make moral absolutes the basis of any foreign policy because he is quite sure that "good and evil can and do exist concurrently in the whole realm of human life."

Fourth, Acheson believes that power and its distribution are crucial elements in world affairs which must be thoroughly considered by the formulators of American foreign policy.

As Acheson looks back on the history of the twentieth century, he sees a kinetic power equilibrium as the chief characteristic of international relations. The crucial center, the "hinge of fate," in this balance of power is the European continent. Even by 1917, Acheson claims, technical advances had changed the Atlantic Ocean from a vast protective moat to an undefended plain reaching to America's shores, making the United States vulnerable to any hostile European power. American participation in both World Wars was a direct result of the domination of Europe by one power, for the destruction of the power balance in Europe presented a direct threat to American national security.

After 1945, Russian pressures on Western Europe made mandatory a powerful counterbalancing system. As it was evident that no such system was possible without active American participation, NATO was formed. And it remains the cornerstone of Western defense against the intrusion of Soviet power. The amalgamation of the power that it represents provides protection to Europe and the United States alike. Acheson believes that the whole future of Western civilization depends on the ability of the NATO alliance to remain strong and adaptable so as to counterbalance the power of the Communist states: ". . . No one believes that the European nations could defend themselves without America; without a dependable Atlantic Alliance they would become hostages to the Soviet Union."[10] It is this fervent belief in the need for a strong United States–Western European interlock which has placed Acheson at odds with General de Gaulle's concept of a Europe of nation-states moving away from America's leadership.

[10] Acheson, "Europe: Decision or Drift," p. 202.

From Acheson's conviction that power can be limited only by countervailing power follows his commitment to an American foreign policy based on strength and power. "Weakness is not strength, and equal power is better than unequal power."[11] It is the responsibility of the United States, as the strongest nation, to assume leadership of the free world in countering the Soviet Union's thrusts. Acheson does not limit his definition of power to force. Rather, he believes power flows from a combination of elements: production rates, natural resources, technology, plant facilities, population, and the intangibles of will and determination. Thus, America's foreign policy should be derived from a power foundation that effectively integrates its financial, political, economic, and military components.

A fifth theme of Acheson's view of international relations is that military force is and will continue to be a major and necessary element in international relations. The West cannot avoid the fact that force or the threat of its use must play a substantial role in the grand strategy of creating a strong and viable non-Communist system. Acheson endorses deterrence strategy as indispensable for blocking the Soviet Union and Communist China from military expansionism. The deterrence strategy of the United States must be flexible, able to operate at all levels of intensity, and adjustable in the amount of force needed for the objectives. In relation to the Vietnam conflict, Acheson has stated that military force must fit into a diplomatic situation so that the North Vietnamese can end the situation "with as less loss of face—as little loss of face—as possible."[12] Since force must be related to the objective desired, it is unthinkable that a nuclear holocaust could result from a miscalculation of intentions or from incapac-

[11] Acheson, "Withdrawal from Europe? 'An Illusion,' " p. 68.

[12] "Mr. Acheson on Ending the War: They Don't Negotiate a Stop," *The National Observer* (December 11, 1967), p. 4.

ity to meet different types of threats. The United States must not be faced with "either/or" situations in force confrontations; its policy makers must never be forced to choose between the pole of surrender and the pole of nuclear war. The military capacity must be an instrument that is, first of all, directed toward avoiding a nuclear war or the acts which might lead to such a war. From the base of credible deterrence, the United States may in fact be able to reach agreement with the Soviet Union in areas where the two nations share a mutual self-interest, for example, in the prevention of obviously accidental nuclear warfare and nuclear proliferation.

Acheson thinks that to unilaterally renounce the use of military force in international affairs is wrong, perhaps even immoral, for it would deny one's own nation a crucial element of power that might be essential for its very survival. He writes:

> Is it moral to deny ourselves the use of force in all circumstances, when our adversaries employ it, under handy excuses, whenever it seems useful to tip the scales of power against every value we think of as moral and as making life worth living?
>
> It seems to me not only a bad bargain, but a stupid one. For the very conception of morality seems to me to involve a duty to preserve values outside the contour of our skins, and at the expense of foregoing much that is desired and pleasant, including—it may be—our own fortunes and lives.[13]

Nevertheless, Acheson denies that in the long run military capability can be substituted for the negotiation of disputes. Military strength is a means of foreign policy; it must never become an end in itself. The United States must never build its military force with the objective of using it—no American purpose can justify a first strike. Time and again, Acheson strikes out against the "massive retaliation" and "first strike" concepts because they

[13] Acheson, "Ethics in International Relations Today," p. 228.

give the impression that the United States might take the initiative in starting a war.

In his writings and speeches, Acheson often concentrates on military factors because he is convinced that military power is the variable in international relations that, in the postwar years, has undergone the most revolutionary change. Old military traditions, he points out, have become outdated: the concepts of unlimited objectives and the use of unlimited force for their achievement are unrealistic in today's world of nuclear weapons. They have been replaced by new military strategies such as limited warfare and guerrilla warfare, which have interlocked the political and military instruments of modern foreign policy so tightly that they are inseparable. "Total victory," "preventive war," and "massive retaliation" are all naive attempts to "kick the problem" of complexities in international relations. Atomic warfare cannot be viewed as a positive element of policy; it is not an instrument of policy. It is the negation of plan and purpose beyond itself. In today's world, when it comes to the use of force and the growth of military capabilities, there can be no bluff since the risks are too great for anything but the most sober and blunt truth.

Acheson's sixth point is that problem solving in the international arena is a perpetually dynamic process. As one problem is solved, a new one takes its place; and new relationships are formed. He is opposed to any rigid policy framework that tries to fit situations or problems into a preconceived pattern. Owing to the shifting and unstable nature of world events, national interests cannot be protected by static arrangements with other nations, whether they be friends or foes. Rather, solutions to international problems must be sought through active decision-making on a step-by-step basis. Policy makers must make a conscious effort: (1) to overcome their predilection to rely on policies which were successful in the past; (2) to avoid indecision and thus forestall the danger that outside pressures will in fact determine foreign policy; and (3) to create a strategic framework which allows for the flexibility needed to adjust to changing situations and changing power relationships.

Decisions, Acheson believes, must be made with consideration of existing power structures and in light of priorities of national interest. Choices in international affairs are rarely between good and evil; often all alternatives are bad. But all can be based on a realistic and flexible approach. In effect Acheson is apprehensive of any rigid policy outlook that neglects allies, promises total solutions, or guarantees certain outcomes.

> One cannot guarantee all . . . results . . . . [T]hose who insist on basing foreign policy on sure things are likely to end up with no policy at all; the test of success in a foreign policy is whether it turns a desired possibility into a probability.[14]

Seventh, Acheson violently objects to historical and philosophical doctrines of inevitability. He sees the free, individual personality as the supreme essence of life. Communist doctrine, in his interpretation, is rooted in the false assumption that history is on a predetermined course. And the Soviet Union and Communist China are adding to the coercive powers of the state the new scientific techniques of mass communications in order to impose a crushing uniformity upon the individuals under their control. Here appears another basic reason for Acheson's "hard" stand against both the ideological dimensions and the operational techniques of the Communist systems.

Acheson believes that man is not a helpless creature who must await an inexorable fate. On the contrary, he is capable of choosing between alternatives within both the national and international spheres. When endowed with exceptional creative pow-

[14] Acheson, *Power and Diplomacy*, p. 22.

ers—intelligence, wisdom, and imagination—he may on occasion even change the course of history. One such person, Acheson points out, was Winston Churchill:

As one uncontrollable force after another has been let loose to propagate still others, man has become more and more the victim of his own creations. Yet Mr. Churchill has been one of the few—the very few—who have significantly and beneficently affected the course of events. That course would have been markedly different without him. . . .
At a time when man has seemed to be dwarfed by his own creations, you [Winston Churchill] have shown us anew the grandeur and greatness which the human spirit can achieve. It is by this that men live.[15]

Individualism, then, is the philosophical foundation of democracy, and can flourish only in an environment of free inquiry and free thought. Any movements (domestic or foreign), doctrines, or institutions that seek to chain man's thinking or to control man's spirit of creation must, therefore, be opposed. All "human institutions are made for man and not man for institutions."[16]

[15] Acheson, *Sketches from Life of Men I Have Known,* p. 84. The quote is from a letter to Winston Churchill at the time of Churchill's retirement from the office of Prime Minister in 1955.

[16] Acheson, *A Democrat Looks at His Party,* p. 45. It is on this very point of Acheson's great respect for man's individual personality that he has been attacked by critics on two counts: (1) he is accused of being a moralist himself by opposing communism on its Stalinist, doctrinal bases. He has not, according to critics, been able to adapt to the changes that have occurred in the Soviet Union's philosophical outlook since the death of Stalin. (2) He was accused, while he was in office, of not being able to separate his public duties from his private friendships, especially in the case of Alger Hiss.

Of course, Acheson has admirers who defend him against these two charges. At the same time, one of the most interesting defenses of Acheson in respect to the Hiss charge comes from an article on quotations

Eighth, Acheson believes an unseverable tie exists between a nation's domestic and international affairs; foreign policy is not and cannot be a disembodied thing. The outward strength of a democracy can be no greater than its inward strength. Only as the United States makes progress at home in achieving the promise of its society by strengthening the foundations of individual freedom, justice, and equality can it demonstrate to the world that democracy is a vital and progressive way of life. The viability of its domestic institutions will in the long run determine the influence that the United States can exert abroad. Americans must realize that in their attitudes toward their neighbors they are helping to decide international issues, in their political struggles they are influencing world events, and the soundness of their domestic economy is inextricably related to the state of the international economy.

It is an intrinsic duty, Acheson concludes, for American policy makers to provide strong, positive leadership that convincingly demonstrates to the American people the interrelationship of national interests and international goals. The American people must be shown that a faith in democracy at home is the prerequisite for instilling faith in democracy to others throughout the world. Maximizing American success in international affairs depends:

> On the unusual leader who has the rare combination of qualities which are needed for successful leadership in a democracy, not only

---

which stresses Acheson's concern for the individual personality as the basis of his "I do not intend to turn my back on Alger Hiss" statement. See Richardson, "Open Letter to John Bartlett," pp. 32–34: "Acheson was much maligned for this statement, but bore the upbraiding with dignity, and the evidence seems to be that instead of meaning to condone what Hiss had done the Secretary's intention was to show that he would not kick a man who was down."

courage and common sense, but that blending of persuasiveness and willingness which can make the unpalatable acceptable.[17]

Ninth, Acheson sees the underdeveloped nations as areas of peripheral concern to the United States, far subordinate to the core area in Western Europe on which, he believes, the survival of the free world depends. Although American policy makers should of course sympathize with the new countries struggling toward political and economic stability, they should also be aware that in any showdown American interests will be best advanced by the former colonial powers. Without Western unity, both Europe and the emerging states would be subject to great danger from Communist propaganda, subversion, and perhaps even invasion. Never, therefore, should the United States publicly condemn its European partners; never must another Suez occur.

In Acheson's view, four postulates should guide American policy toward the new nations of Asia, Africa, and Latin America:

1. Unlike contemporary nationalist movements, the American Revolution was a political act and not a social revolution. Therefore, the United States should refrain from active participation in the internal affairs of the emerging nations, not only because of the obvious difficulties of any intervention, but also because it is philosophically unidentified with this new type of revolution.

2. Freedom and democracy require that a certain level of national economic productivity exist within a state, for freedom is a fragile thing that withers under the stress of economic privation or crisis. Therefore, economic and military foreign aid should be concentrated in those states where American interjection of the missing component carries promise that democratic systems will be established.

3. The revolutionary nationalism of the new nations inevi-

[17] Acheson, *Power and Diplomacy,* pp. 27–28.

tably sets up new dynamics and new sources of power that must adapt to the prevailing power patterns. It is a responsibility of the United States to see that this adjustment occurs in a peaceful manner, and to avoid the chaos which is so profitable to Communism. But as the United States works against military aggression and economic disarray, it must, on the other hand, never oppose change itself. Alliances, foreign aid, and international institutions all offer means to assimilate the new countries into a stable international environment.

4. National self-interest must be a major American guideline in its relations with the emerging nations. The United States, according to Acheson, should not be swept away by humanitarian sentiments. Instead of instituting a generalized welfare program for all the new nations, it should aid specific nations for specific purposes within the capacity of its resources. To the emerging nations themselves falls the responsibility for demonstrating some political stability and economic determination before receiving United States aid.

Tenth, and finally, Acheson, though he is loath to base the ends of foreign policy on a moral basis, still feels that:

> an area in our foreign relations where guidance from what is excellent in conduct may be more confidently sought than in some others . . . is in the methods by which foreign relations are conducted.[18]

In fact, he is convinced that the methods by which international relations are conducted are as important as the nation-states' goals themselves. In their negotiations, diplomats should be straightforward, candid, honorable, and courageous. This in itself can encourage stability. It can also do much to diminish the tendency to regard the art of diplomacy as the stratagem of going to the verge of war to accomplish a purpose.

[18] Acheson, "Morality, Moralism, and Diplomacy," p. 491.

Acheson urges the United States to take the lead in conducting diplomacy at the highest possible ethical level:

There should be no bullying, no advantage taken of the hardship of others to drive political bargains, no lying or boasting in our propaganda or our dealings with others, no sanctimonious lecturing of others or their faults, no consciousness of our own effortless righteousness, or the thanking of God that we are not as other men.[19]

Diplomats, through ethical approaches to international problems, decrease the chance of war arising from miscalculation or misunderstanding, while attaining a flexibility that allows compromises based on self-interest. Consequently, the methods of traditional diplomacy are at the very roots in the attempt to find agreeable solutions to the tensions in the international arena.

And yet, Acheson has no illusions about what diplomacy can accomplish in today's world. For example, when asked a question by a student concerning the chances of the United States negotiating its way out of Vietnam, Acheson stated:

Too many people have a completely wrong idea of negotiation as conceived of by the Communists and as conceived of by us, a different idea. With us, negotiation is a David Harum business in which both parties want to reach a result and each one wants to get a slight advantage in reaching a predetermined result—sale of a horse, end of war—whatever it may be. The Communists have a Clausewitz idea toward negotiation . . . negotiation is war carried on by other means, and what they hope to do in a negotiation is not to bring about a peace, but to disadvantage somebody in the course of a war, separate you from your allies, cause you domestic trouble at home, and so forth.[20]

[19] *Ibid.*, p. 493.

[20] "Mr. Acheson on Ending the War: They Don't Negotiate a Stop," p. 3.

Therefore, even while trying to improve diplomatic methods, American policy makers must remain conscious of international realities.

Acheson's insights into international relations display elements of both cynicism and optimism. On the one hand, he firmly rejects the idea that man will ever live under a supranational world government based on universal law and decency. On the other hand, he is convinced that man can resist tyranny and conformity through the use of his creative intelligence. Hard work on immediate problems and the adoption of sound methods of diplomatic intercourse will protect the world from nuclear holocaust until some day in the future when broader negotiations may be undertaken. Acheson's hopes for international relations in the future are inextricably entwined with his view of the present. His favorite quotation in relation to international affairs seems to be the statement made by Andrew Jackson to his troops at New Orleans—"Elevate them guns a little lower."[21] This, in effect, is Acheson's message to the American foreign-policy makers of today, policy makers who must stand with one foot in the world of hopes for future order among nations and with the other foot in the world of tension and strife of the present.

[21] In this same vein, Acheson has other favorite quotations; for example, (1) Lincoln's caution to beware of "pernicious abstractions," (2) The golf quote: "Keep your head down, and your eye on the ball," and (3) Secretary of State Marshall's statement, "Don't fight the problem, decide it!"

CHAPTER FOUR

The Secretary of State as Department Head

Dean Acheson sees the Department of State as the foundation from which the Secretary of State must operate in order to maximize his influence and effectiveness in the foreign-policy process.[1] The elements of organization, personnel, and information must be carefully blended to assure that the Secretary can operate with knowledge and authority as both a policy initiator and a Presidential adviser. And this can be accomplished only if the Secretary of State himself takes an active and interested part in administering the Department. To optimize the potentials of the Department, the Secretary must encourage its personnel to be active, creative, and thought-

[1] Acheson, "What a Secretary of State Really Does," p. 48.

ful participants in the policy-making process. For the Secretary of State cannot bring facts and information of the highest quality to bear on foreign-policy problems without full confidence that his people in the Department are producing at the peak of their capabilities. Acheson has written:

> As a maker and executor of foreign policy, whatever the appearances, the Secretary of State is not an individual performer. He is part of an institution, another essential part of which is the personnel of the Department of State and the Foreign Service from which flow to him his initial analyses of problems and recommendations for dealing with them.[2]

As noted in the first chapter, the State Department has grown enormously in terms of staff, paperwork, and responsibility. It has become a complicated and complex decisional unit that is difficult for one man to control and direct. Acheson has been quoted as saying: "Nobody has been able to run the Department in a hundred and fifty years."[3] Yet, certain Secretaries have obviously been more effective than others in galvanizing the huge agency into an efficient policy-making unit. Some have profited from the power of their own personalities (George Marshall); some from intimate relationships with the President (John Foster Dulles); and others from the pressures of internal or external crises (William Seward). Dean Acheson was one of the best at keeping the Department operating at a high level of administrative efficiency and policy innovation; his success is attributable to a mixture of ingredients: personal stature, institutional experience, and Presidential confidence.

President Truman nominated Dean Acheson to be his Secretary of State because of Acheson's long experience in the State Department, first as Assistant Secretary and then as Under Secre-

[2] Acheson, *A Democrat Looks at His Party*, p. 159.
[3] Quoted in McCamy, *Conduct of the New Diplomacy*, p. 7.

tary. To the attribute of professional competence, Acheson adds three other criteria for the selection of Secretaries of State: the President must pick a man in whom he has complete confidence and trust; the appointee must be able gracefully to fit into the prevailing international environment; and the appointee should not be someone who overshadows the President in stature or popularity.

Once the new Secretary of State assumes office, he must perform three major Departmental roles, contends Acheson, if the Department is to function at top efficiency. First is a corporate role: the administration and management of the Department. Second is a policy-making role: guidance and participation within the Department of the policy-making process. And third is a representative role: presentation of the State Department's policy suggestions and corporate interests in the larger policy-making arena of the national government. None of these roles can be ignored if the Secretary is to have a 100 percent effort by his departmental colleagues, nor can any substantial imbalance of attention occur. To assure a functional decision unit of high quality, the Secretary must attend to each role and harmonize all three, though he may at times, due to the pressures of events or personalities, be forced to concentrate more on one than the others.

The intra-Departmental roles of the Secretary are obviously related; however, for the sake of in-depth analysis each will be examined separately.

In his corporate role, the Secretary of State must prove to his colleagues, his peers, and the President that he is operationally, not just figuratively, the director of his organization. Acheson is convinced that to achieve this end, Departmental control must be centralized in the office of the Secretary. While he was Secretary, he worked hard and successfully for passage of the reorganization act of May 26, 1949, which transferred to the Secretary administrative powers previously wielded by the Assistant Secretary for Administration and the Director General of the Foreign Service. It is not that Acheson feels that the Secretary should oversee all routine administrative procedures, but rather that he should personally set the guidelines and patterns within which his subordinates operate.

In order for a Secretary of State to extract from his department its fullest potential, states Acheson, he must defend the professionalism of his "soldiers."[4] From the lowest to the top levels, Department workers must be able to depend on the Secretary to protect them from outside pressures. Good morale and high standards of performance could not otherwise be expected.

Also indispensable is the presence of an administrative assistant who is professionally capable of coordinating the organizational problems of the internal policy-making process. In 1950, Acheson, in stating his great respect for Under Secretary of State James Webb (who was his major administrative coordinator in the State Department), emphasized the Secretary's need for administrative experts to have an efficient team:

> I do not know of any man in the entire United States . . . who has greater genius for organization, a genius for understanding how to take a great mass of people and bring them together; so that he pulls out of them all the knowledge and all the competence that they have; so that each person is doing what he ought to be doing; so that efforts of this vast group are pulled together to get a tremendously powerful result. And that is absolutely essential in the Department of State.

Acheson sees no organizational panacea for solving the prob-

[4] During an interview with Mr. Acheson on April 14, 1966, it was interesting to note that he referred to his State Department colleagues as "soldiers." This seems to substantiate the fact that Mr. Acheson views the national policy-making arena much the same as he views the international arena; that is, in the context of a struggle syndrome.

lems of American foreign relations, but he strongly believes that a coordinated, centralized administrative structure is a prerequisite to the process of effective policy formation.

The second role of the Secretary of State is that of fostering within the Department formulations of policy alternatives. Acheson is convinced that the Department will generate fresh and imaginative ideas only if staff members are assured that their ideas are welcomed and used. Hence, a Secretary of State must be an ardent leader and advocate in order to maintain the morale and creativity of his colleagues.

In regard to ideas and organization in the Department's policymaking process, Acheson has said:

> . . . it had been my experience that thought was not of much use without knowledge and guidance, and that who should give me both and how competent they would be must depend on who chose, dealt with, assigned, and promoted those people and established the forms of organization within which they worked. All this seemed a precondition of thinking which I could not ignore if my thoughts were going to amount to anything.[5]

It is impossible for any Secretary of State to spin thoughts and policies out of his viscera as spiders spin their webs. Policy alternatives must come "bubbling up" from the lower levels. One method of encouraging this process is for the Secretary of State to delegate authority to his subordinates to freely pursue specific problems. On April 22, 1950, while speaking to the American Society of Newspaper Editors, Acheson said:

> I don't sit behind them and pull their coattails or look over their shoulders. I am kept informed by the central secretariat, of anything that happens. I am permitted to get in, if I wish to, before something is done. . . .
>
> [W]e have carried out a reorganization which is based on these men

[5] Acheson, "Thoughts About Thought in High Places," p. 291.

being the operators of the State Department. They are not people who sit around and argue with one another. Each one of them is responsible for carrying out a job, and the policy under which he carried it out is worked out through the planning staff, with the cooperation of all these men. The policy is laid down and they are given their authority.

Within the context of his intra-institutional policy-making role, the Secretary of State must at various times perform as initiator, participant, and judge. Particularly in crisis situations (e.g., Korean aggression, Cuban missile crisis), the Secretary may be called upon to participate in the initiation of policy in *ad hoc* groups. This is a delicate operation that requires considerable tact if it is to be accepted with enthusiasm by his Departmental subordinates. First, he must be sure that the Department is fully aware of his general orientation toward world affairs so that his colleagues will be able to identify his individual stamp on each crisis policy. Second, he must make clear to his staff that his methods in crisis-type decisions are "deviations of necessity" from his usual policy-making patterns; never must the Department feel that the Secretary habitually makes policies off the cuff. And finally, the Secretary must have attained a firm reputation as both an idea man and a foreign-affairs professional to assure that when he does participate in the initiation of a crisis policy, his people will know that he has utilized the information passed up to him from below.[6] Recognizing the Secretary as a responsible leader, his colleagues will then see that crisis decisions are executed quickly and efficiently within the Department.

Acheson believes that the Secretary's participation in the insti-

[6] Interview with Acheson, April 14, 1966; Elder, *The Policy Machine,* pp. 73, 86–87. Mr. Elder points out the importance of the Policy Planning Staff in helping Acheson, while he was Secretary of State, to relate short-range problems to long-range objectives.

tutional policy-making process is another vehicle that can elicit the "inspired best" from his colleagues. His participation can be direct, by personal presence, or indirect, by measured and intelligent reactions to candid policy suggestions from his staff. In either case, the Secretary of State must adopt an operational pattern in which his subordinates feel free to be frank and creative in their policy suggestions. In summary, to ensure the flow of policy suggestions up through the hierarchical levels within the Department: (1) he must protect and raise the morale of his soldiers; (2) he must reward great effort and excellence, and at the same time condemn mediocrity "picturesquely" (the "carrot and stick" method); (3) he must make sure that the organizational structure is flexible enough so that policy ideas can be readily filtered to the highest departmental levels; and (4) he must personally choose trusted, knowledgeable and candid advisers for his staff.[7]

Time and again, Acheson stresses the Secretary's "judicial character" in the policy process within the State Department. Acheson advances three procedures indispensable for the successful functioning of the Secretary as "judge": (1) as policy alternatives filter to the top, the Secretary must weigh their merits and make the final decision as to which is the best course for the Department to pursue. (2) Before reaching a final decision, the Secretary must supplement his reading of predigested memos with analysis based on thoughtful contemplation. (3) To eliminate the possibility of someone being overlooked in the oral transmission of policy decisions, he must make certain that his final decisions are written ones and that they are transmitted in black and white to all concerned Department personnel.[8]

[7] All four points were made by Mr. Acheson in an interview conducted on April 14, 1966. In addition, this pattern was corroborated in interviews with Paul H. Nitze and Carlton Savage.

[8] Acheson, "The President and the Secretary of State," p. 41; interview with Acheson, April 14, 1966.

Acheson's own policy-making pattern while he was Secretary of State, as reported by Philip Hamburger, clearly demonstrates the judicial facet of his role in the departmental process:

Leaning far back in his red leather chair, taking notes in pencil, he listens to each man's exposition of his conception of the problem and his suggested remedy. Occasionally Acheson asks a question but he rarely expresses an opinion until everyone else in the room has had his say. He then summarizes what he has heard, points out the conflicts between the several points of view, attempts to reconcile them, and finally offers a solution based on the other men's opinions and his own. "His summations are much on the order of those of a fine judge charging a jury."[9]

In the context of his role as a representative, Acheson perceives the duty of the Secretary of State to include performances before five essential audiences: the American people; the diplomats of other nations, especially the Western Allies; other executive agencies; Congress; and the President. The Secretary must stand as the symbol of the State Department before the American people. A Secretary who shows courage in the face of criticism, who articulates the Department's proposals with precision and clarity, and who emphasizes the corporate, institutional nature of his position does more than help to educate the American public: he solidifies the support of colleagues by sharing vicariously his triumphs and tragedies within the American political process. A "team man" spirit in the Secretary's public presentations encourages his subordinates to confidence in his leadership.[10]

[9] Hamburger, "Profiles: Mr. Secretary, I," p. 46.

[10] Interview with Acheson, April 14, 1966. A danger of performing this symbolic role before the American people is that a Secretary of State may, at times, try to separate his individual personality from his institutional personality to the detriment of his colleagues. This is one of the

The Secretary of State must demonstrate to the diplomats of other nations a professional negotiating ability and a leadership status in the "coalition diplomacy" among the Western nations in order to reinforce his internal position in the Department. As he performs with dignity and courage and as he produces acceptable agreements, his colleagues will do their best to meet his demands for diplomatic materials. Their devotion, moreover, will spill over into other, traditional diplomatic areas of the administration of foreign policy.

Third, he must be prepared to fight to protect the role of the Secretary and the State Department as the President's principal advisers on foreign policies from intrusion of other executive agencies, established or new. No organizational layer between the President and Secretary of State can be tolerated. Thus Acheson has been particularly opposed to any attempts to give the National Security Council (NSC) more power or formal structure in the policy-making arena. He believes that structured interdepartmental committees such as the NSC both cut down the flexibility within the policy-making process and intrude upon the highly personal relationship needed between a President and his Secretary of State. Even worse, they produce policy recommendations based on "agreement by exhaustion," as the large committees strain mightily to produce, not clear-cut analyses of alternate courses, but broad compromises or carefully concealed "plasterings over" of differences.

The Secretary of State must also protect his colleagues from Congressional attempts to penetrate into the internal policy-making process of the State Department, especially when

---

interpretations of the "Hiss Affair" during Acheson's tenure as Secretary of State. In other words, his personal friendships with the Hiss brothers were said, by some, to have been carried too far by Mr. Acheson while he was the institutional leader of the State Department.

"witch-hunting" Congressmen ask questions such as "Who was responsible for certain policy recommendations and who was against them?" This type of information must never be released to Congressmen; it is imperative that the Secretary of State let Congress know as clearly as possible that he, as Department head, takes full responsibility for the decisions and policies released from his Department. Through his firm stand, the Secretary reaps a number of benefits for himself and for his Department. His colleagues within the Department will not fear to be candid in their policy recommendations to the Secretary. The President's confidence in his Secretary of State will be reinforced by the knowledge that the Secretary is receiving undistilled information and advice from within his Department, and also by the evidence that the Secretary is a staunch defender of executive primacy in the formulation of foreign policy. Congressmen who want to make political gains at the expense of the State Department will be discouraged from seeking individual "whipping boys" on whom they can unleash their wrath. Finally, the Secretary, by drawing the fire onto himself, will gain respect in the eyes of his subordinates and his peers, both for his courage and for his assignment as the authoritative, formal spokesman for the Department's policies before Congress. Acheson frankly believes that a Secretary of State should be proud to bear the scars of congressional battles that are inflicted as he defends his soldiers against congressional attack.

The need for the Secretary of State to guard against congressional inroads on Departmental prerogatives is not only administrative; it is also functional. The Secretary must make sure that Congress recognizes that it is the State Department, not the legislative branch of government, which is the center of foreign-policy formulation. When the Eisenhower Administration assumed office, Acheson lamented, ". . . . It was not at all clear who was going to furnish American leadership—Mr. Dulles and the State

Department or Senator McCarthy and Messrs. Cohn and Shine."

To Acheson, the most important representative role that the Secretary performs for the Department is in relation to the President. The Secretary must present to the President the views of his Department, and then he must "fight like hell" to have his recommendations accepted by the President as national policy. Only if the Secretary of State can score a high ratio of policy acceptances *vis-à-vis* the suggestions of other policy units, can he extract a maximum effort from his colleagues. Acheson thus maintains that there is a direct correlation between the Secretary's representative role with the President and the quantity and quality of policy suggestions presented to him by his departmental colleagues.[11]

Acheson has no doubt that each new President is suspicious of the personnel in the State Department. He also believes that most State Department professionals, especially the Foreign Service officers, are equally apprehensive of a new President until they find out for sure how he intends to operate in regard to the Department. Acheson is convinced that the Secretary of State is thus confronted with a bifurcated problem that must be handled with great tact and sophistication. On the one hand, he must protect his soldiers from Presidential pressures stemming from distrust, while he reassures his subordinates that the President intends to utilize the Department as his primary formulator of foreign-policy alternatives. Only by the most conscientious effort to close this "suspicion gap" can a Secretary of State ensure a high quality policy-making effort by his Departmental colleagues and persuade the President to make maximum use of the State Department.

As was observed above, the three roles of the Secretary of

[11] Interview with Acheson, April 14, 1966; Acheson, "The President and the Secretary of State," p. 40.

State—corporate, policy making, and representative—are often so intertwined as to be inseparable. Those who execute policy have a great influence on its formation; policy formulators are dependent on the administrative organization; no policies can be effective without skilled representation to the public, diplomatic circles, Congress, and the President; yet the finest public relations cannot substitute for intelligent decision-making. A review of some of the attitudes of Acheson toward McCarthyism will emphasize the interdependence of the Secretary's duties.

Unless the professionalism of the Department's personnel is protected from outside intervention, Acheson contends, the result will be a fragmented policy-making organization operating from a base of fear, hesitation, and disillusion. Acheson therefore has urged Secretaries of State to take strong stands against scapegoat hunts (e.g., McCarthyism) and congressional bullying. To counter such phenomena as McCarthyism, a Secretary of State must protect his colleagues from two levels of attack—the individual, personal level and the policy-making, utility level. Acheson is appalled at the efforts of any outside group to further its own personal or political ambitions through character assassinations of individual Department members. To Acheson, the methods of McCarthyism smacked of totalitarianism, a denial of the worth of the individual personality which Acheson so cherishes. A Secretary must make every effort to see that his subordinates are protected as individuals against irresponsible outside accusations. When he departed as Secretary of State he said:

> One thing I think you are entitled to ask, and, again, if you have not received that you are entitled to ask that you should not be vilified; that your loyalty should not be brought in doubt; that slanders and libel should not be made against you.[12]

[12] "Secretary Acheson's Farewell to His Colleagues," *The Department of State Bulletin,* 28, No. 709 (January 26, 1953), p. 161.

But Acheson sees the Secretary of State's duty as going far beyond the need to prevent the vilification of individuals. The Secretary must also protect his colleagues for a utilitarian purpose; to preserve the Department of State as an important policy-making organization. Whenever scapegoat hunts such as McCarthyism have been allowed to penetrate the Department, its staff has become more cautious, more afraid to formulate new ideas or to question traditional policies. In Acheson's opinion, any investigation "exercised under an obsession with security, with fear of the unconventional, the diverse point of view, . . . brings stagnation and timidity."[13] For the sake of the Department too, the Secretary of State must do all in his power to shield his subordinates from the likes of McCarthy and, going further, must actively fight any movements which seek to sow the seeds of hysteria and distrust toward his people.

To produce the highest possible quality of policy alternatives, the State Department must be entirely free from the threat of secret trials, enforced conformity, or personality purges. If errors of judgment become equated to security risks and the Secretary of State receives nothing but watered-down, vague recommendations from his subordinates, his ability to inform the President would be seriously impaired and the demise of the State Department as an effective policy-making unit would be imminent. The Secretary must do all within his power to protect the Department from such attacks—including drawing the fire of its opponents to himself.[14] One of Acheson's most explicit complaints about the methods of McCarthyism concerned the bypassing of the Foreign Service Board, whose members had full knowledge of the standards required of Foreign Service officers. He deplored the fact that the critical and damaging findings against Foreign Service officers (e.g. John Paton Davies) were uncovered by

[13] Acheson, *A Democrat Looks at His Party,* p. 161.
[14] *Ibid,* pp. 158–161.

ad hoc boards that were composed of persons who had no professional knowledge of the standard required of Foreign Service officers or of the foreign-policy problems under which they condemned the officer's judgment, discretion, and reliability.

In summation, Acheson is convinced that the Secretary of State must perform the roles of initiator, participant, and representative, in order to keep the State Department functioning at top efficiency. And in seeking to fulfill his function as a policy maker, a Secretary of State is doomed to failure if he ignores the advice of his colleagues and attempts to "go it alone" in his recommendations to the President. A Secretary is only as effective as the quality and foresight of his Department.

CHAPTER FIVE

The Relations of the Secretary of State with the President and the Executive Agencies

The success of a Secretary of State is inseparably linked to his personal relationship with the President. When there is a firm and steady rapport between the Secretary and his Chief Executive, the power of the Secretary is enhanced throughout the policy-making arena. As coordinator, synthesizer, and initiator, he will function more freely and effectively. And he will be able to protect his department from incursions by other agencies into the foreign-policy processes. Thus, Acheson is convinced that the first order of business of any Secretary of State is to establish close and cordial working associations with the President.

The Acheson operational code, therefore, bases a considerable segment of its superstructure on the undergriding of the President–Secretary of State relationship. The methods and procedures that a Secretary employs in gaining the President's confidence are the linchpins which hold together the operational framework. Acheson attempts to demonstrate how this relationship is affected by the style, personality, and operating procedures of the two men. These characteristics, in turn, relate to other Presidential advisers, executive department heads, and interdepartmental committees. Acheson's perceptions of these phenomena will clarify both the interpersonal and inter-institutional facets of the policy-making process that must be dealt with by any Secretary of State.

Above all else, the Secretary must prove to the President that he merits the position of chief adviser on foreign policy, that he and his colleagues within the State Department are eminently qualified to lead in the formulation and execution of the Administration's program. To ensure his leading role, the Secretary must operate on three levels: personal (subjective relationship), institutional (structural relationship), and operational (professional relationship).

A Secretary must work hard to cultivate an intensely personal relationship with his chief, for from a cordial and harmonious association will emerge the common support and mutual loyalty indispensable to fulfillment of the objectives of the Secretary. The Secretary must be fully aware of the President's temperament, character, and operating methods; and must adapt his own style to them. The President–Secretary of State relationship Acheson believes, involves particular men, not abstract principles, and must be re-formed for each new set of personalities. Acheson and Truman established an almost ideal relationship of mutual respect and admiration. On his departure from office, Acheson stressed its importance to him as Secretary of State:

It was in this chair [Acheson's cabinet chair] that I sought to bring him [President Truman] all the help and support and loyalty of which I am capable. And it is sitting there that I have received from him that unswerving support and loyalty without which no one in my position can ever hope truly to serve his country . . .[1]

But more than affection and loyalty is needed between the Secretary and the Chief Executive. The President must also be confident of his Secretary's abilities as a foreign policy professional. The Secretary must demonstrate the personal capacity to think more and more deeply than others about the nation's needs and interests, as a state among states, in a world of change and movement and of unparalleled danger. He will then be listened to as the "first among equals" in the foreign-policy process. In addition to being a candid, creative, and knowledgeable adviser to the President, the Secretary of State should be an advocate. He must not merely persuade the President, but press him with all the means at his command to use the Presidential influence, authority, and command to accept policy recommendations from the Secretary and the State Department. There is no place in Acheson's thinking for a Secretary unwilling to fight for measures he judges beneficial to the national interests of the United States. The Secretary can give the President complete personal loyalty without the need to hide his own convictions during the period of policy formulation.

The Secretary must always remember, however, that once the President has made his final decision, the Secretary must give it his complete support. Under the Constitution, the President is assigned primary responsibility for directing the foreign relations of the American people; the Secretary of State is appointed by the President to assist him in this task. This hierarchical, formal relationship must be mutually recognized at the very outset of their affiliation. No doubt must exist that the Office of the Secretary is the junior partner of the Presidential office; no doubt

[1] "Secretary Acheson's Farewell to His Colleagues," p. 161.

must exist that the President is the final arbiter in the policy process; no doubt must exist that the President's decisions will be faithfully executed by the Secretary, regardless of his personal judgments. When Senator Millard Tydings asked Acheson at the hearings on his nomination for Secretary of State in 1949 what he would do as Secretary should he be unable to accept the foreign-policy course that the President was suggesting, Acheson answered, "I anticipate nothing so unhappy . . . . But should it arise, I would resign."[2]

Quick recognition of the hierarchical pattern of priorities and execution increases the chances of the Secretary of State to retain both his formal and informal positions as the President's chief adviser on external affairs. Any deviation from their assigned roles, as history has shown, only causes trouble for both individuals:

> Diversions from this pattern have almost always produced bad results —whether it is a Secretary who wants to assume the role of the President (Seward) or a President who believes that either his or the Secretary's responsibilities can be delegated (for example, to the Operations Coordination Board of late unhappy pre-1961 memory).[3]

Although he must never conceive of himself as the President's Prime Minister in charge of foreign affairs, neither must a Secretary become simply a "clerk"—a manager of an executive department.[4] He must seek a middle place in the continuum of responsibility. To avoid the trap of relegation to the status of a

[2] Quoted in "Satisfactory Answers," *Time,* 53 No. 4 (January 24, 1949), p. 15.

[3] Acheson, "Review of *Shaping the Future: Foreign Policy in an Age of Transition* by Robert Bowie," p. 436.

[4] Acheson, "The President and the Secretary of State," p. 33. In addition, see Neustadt, *Presidential Power, the Politics of Leadership,* Chapter 1. The Neustadt book discusses the "leader vs. clerk concepts" in relation to the Presidency. Acheson analyzes the role of the Secretary of State in much the same context.

diplomatic bureaucrat, the Secretary must accentuate his personal competence and avoid being submerged in a morass of administrative mechanisms that would institutionalize his relations with the President. For "insofar as this relationship is attenuated or institutionalized—or Parkinsonized—" its intimacy is threatened by intervening factors.[5]

By a combination of competence, discretion, and devotion, therefore, a Secretary of State may ensure his position as the President's personal adviser on foreign-policy problems. Indeed informal, intangible factors may outweigh his institutional position as head of an executive department in determining his stature in the eyes of the President. A Secretary who conspicuously establishes himself as a personal advocate of the President's foreign policy, an informal protector of the President as an individual, and a partisan in support of the Administration's general legislative program has achieved the basic essentials for effective performance of his role.

In the operation of the policy-making process, the President's personal confidence in his Secretary of State can become solidified. The administrative pattern of policy making, the personal policy-making style of the President, and the ability of the Secretary of State to present the President with candid and comprehensive advice will influence the amount of confidence the President will repose in his Secretary. Acheson outlines specific functions and procedures that will elevate the stature of a Secretary of State as an operating participant in the foreign-policy process:

1. The Secretary of State must be an ardent defender of the Presidential prerogative in foreign affairs and of a strong President. By supporting the President's supremacy in foreign affairs on legal, practical, and political grounds, the Secretary in effect accentuates the importance of the formal position of the Sec-

[5] Acheson, "The Presidency and the Secretary of State," p. 37.

retary of State relative to other branches of government and other executive department heads. Nor will the benefits be limited to the American policy process; they will also extend to his activities in the international diplomatic arena.

Strong Presidential leadership is necessary not only for a consistent and sustained effort in pursuing American interests in international relations, but also for establishing general, long-range policy goals which can clearly be identified by State Department personnel. Once the end is perceived, the exploration by the Department of policy alternatives and the execution of policy decisions will be more imaginative and efficient. Moreover, a President who will take final and definite responsibility for all major foreign-policy decisions forces the Secretary of State to keep his department operating at a high level of quality.

The growth in the magnitude and hazards of foreign-policy decisions in a time of swiftly recurring crises demands that a President have both the courage and the ability to act quickly and decisively. The United States must never be caught short due to lack of Presidential resolve. When the President, in times of crisis, is called upon to make decisions, he must not be hampered by an elaborate, rigid policy process. A Secretary of State must also be able to act decisively in crisis situations so that the President will turn to him for advice and include him in the final decision-making process. By encouraging the President to assume command, the Secretary of State reflects his confidence both in the President's decision-making capacities and in his own individual abilities to operate under stress.

Politically, the President is the leader of the nation. Constitutionally, he is the director of American foreign policy. However, as Acheson points out, these powers of the President are not self-executing;[6] they are determined by the man in the office. It therefore becomes important that the Secretary of State support

[6] Acheson, "The Responsibility for Decision in Foreign Policy," pp. 4–5.

and encourage the President to expand his competence to the fullest. Congress and private-interest groups must not intrude recklessly into the foreign policy-making process if the Secretary of State and his department are to make their maximum contribution to wise and timely decisions. The President weakens the position of the Secretary of State in the foreign-policy process by inviting Congress to organize it for him, or by expecting Congress to share with him the responsibility of policy decisions. The Secretary of State must, for his own benefit, be a fervent supporter of the Presidential prerogative in the area of foreign relations.

2. The Secretary of State must serve as a principal information channel to the President on foreign affairs. Since information is correlated with power in Washington, Acheson contends that the Secretary of State must perform this function in order to solidify his own status. He must brief the President on all matters of foreign policy on a regular and confidential basis. He must see the President often—at least several times a week. And he must brief the President alone. Only then can the two men discuss the complicated matters of foreign policy candidly and in depth.

Acheson's own operating procedures for keeping President Truman fully informed could serve as a model for other Secretaries of State. He saw the President in private about four times a week and he communicated with the President daily through private dispatches when he was away from the Capitol at conferences. Whenever it was possible, he brought up important matters of foreign policy with the President mainly in small groups. Acheson has often disparaged the participation of many people in the policy-making process. Even the Cabinet, he contends, is a clumsy implement.

> The Cabinet is usually a poor place in which to take up an important and complicated matter with the President. Too many uninformed people are likely to get involved and confuse matters.[7]

[7] Acheson, *Morning and Noon,* p. 185.

3. The Secretary of State must be the chief adviser to the President on foreign-policy matters. The Secretary of State, Acheson emphasizes, must give the President the best and most frank advice of which he is capable. He must not tolerate methods or procedures in the foreign-policy process that present the President with watered-down policy alternatives. Since the President is the "decider-in-chief," the greatest service that the Secretary of State can render to his President is to sharpen issues and to make him aware of disagreements, not to cover up different ideas within the executive branch.

The Secretary should not be alarmed if the President seeks advice from other quarters, but should protect his position as first adviser by frank, forthright, and vigorous counsel. His reward will be an intimate knowledge of the President's thought on any situation and the opportunity to advance his own recommendations right up until the time of final Presidential decision.[8]

4. The Secretary of State must act as arbiter between the President and the State Department. Acheson is convinced that there is a high correlation between a President's confidence in his Secretary of State and the Secretary's ability to have the President's final policy decisions implemented with dispatch and efficiency by his department. The Secretary must demonstrate to the President that the State Department is an integrated institution subject to Presidential demands and responsive to changing situations. He must both reflect the views of the President to his colleagues within the department and bring to the President (and his own peers on the top policy-making echelons) the views of his staff. He must fight for policies when he thinks the President or other advisers are mistaken; he must also convince the President that any final policy decision he makes will be fully implemented by his department. By maintaining this delicate balance, the Secre-

[8] Acheson, "What a Secretary of State Really Does," p. 48.

tary of State will persuade the President that his institutional loyalty will never come to dominate his personal loyalty to the President and to the President's foreign-policy directives.

5. The Secretary of State must actively participate in the formulation of Presidential foreign-policy speeches. To be included as a member of the President's speech-writing team is important because this is often where policy is made, regardless of where it is supposed to be made. "The Secretary," says Acheson, "if he is wise, will join the fray himself, with his own draft, and try to guide and direct it."[9] As head of the Department, he carries more weight than any of his subordinates or colleagues throughout the drafting process, but his presence is especially needed in the final stages when the President himself joins the group to make final decisions.

6. The Secretary of State must be an opponent of over-institutionalization in the policy process. Over-institutionalization must be resisted by the Secretary, since it may either diminish the President's flexibility or create a hierarchical barrier between the Secretary of State and his President. For example, in 1954, Acheson stated:

> ... however he works, the President must be free to choose the methods most suited to him. He cannot be confined by law. Legislation that a President must consult this, that, or the other person or body will be futile and harmful. He can be given facilities, but he cannot be compelled to use them.[10]

When interdepartmental committee meetings such as those of the National Security Council are unavoidable, Acheson insists that the Secretary of State or someone from the State Department should chair their discussions, and that recommendations should be presented to the the President by the Secretary himself.

[9] Acheson, "The President and the Secretary of State," p. 44.
[10] Acheson, "The Responsibility for Decision in Foreign Policy," p. 8.

7. The Secretary of State should be a habitual resident of Washington. As was mentioned earlier, Acheson chose to stay close to his staff and the President when he was Secretary of State. "Authority fades with distance and with the speed of light," he contends, and the gains from foreign appearances are usually more than offset by losses from the Secretary's failure actively to take part in the making of foreign-policy decisions.

8. The Secretary of State must be an effective diplomat. Acheson observes that a Secretary of State will gain influence with the President and in the foreign-policy process if he demonstrates courage, honesty, and ability as a negotiator. The confidence of America's allies and the respect of America's antagonists are indicators to the President of the Secretary of State's professional abilities and will add to his role in major foreign-policy decisions.

In summation, the Secretary of State must pursue an operational pattern that blends favorably with that of the President's. To retain his traditional position as the President's foremost adviser on foreign policy, there are many demands upon the person and time of a Secretary of State. He must strive, on the personal level, to be the alter ego of the President; he must recognize, on the institutional level, that his office is subordinate to that of the Presidency; and he must procure, on the operational policy-making level, the President's confidence in his personal abilities and his professional judgments. If a Secretary of State can establish such a pattern, the chances are that he will not be displaced as the President's preeminent adviser on foreign policy.

The success of the Secretary of State in coordinating foreign-policy activities of the State Department with those of other departments, agencies, and personalities, also is dependent on the Secretary's relationship with the President. When the Secretary is convinced that he will be backed by the President in a majority of conflicts with rival agencies and people, he will usually be able to settle disputes by exploiting his own prestige.[11] But if it is evident that other advisers can undercut the Secretary of State, or if other departments have their recommendations accepted by the President over the Secretary's strenuous objections, then the Secretary's power as the principal foreign-policy coordinator is continually challenged and questioned.

In addition to securing Presidential support, Acheson finds that the Secretary of State must struggle to retain a position of preeminence in the foreign-policy process.[12] A number of operating procedures and techniques that will improve the power position of the Secretary of State in relation to other Presidential advisers and executive departments must be undertaken and perfected. First, the Secretary of State must recognize that smooth interdepartmental relations are not established by any automatic procedure. They can develop only through close working arrangements with the other executive department heads within the Administration. The pattern of cooperation established at the top levels within the Administration is especially important, since it determines the style of interaction between departmental personnel all the way down the line.

Second, the Secretary of State must attempt to keep interdepartmental meetings small and informal. Flexibility in the policymaking process, protection of the protean quality that allows quick adjustment to crisis situations, must not be weakened by rigid organizational procedures and institutional structures. Otherwise, the Secretary of State and other department heads would face the possibility of becoming parliamentarians rather than policy makers. A peripheral danger of an elaborate policymaking structure is that permanent bureaucratic officers, such

[11] Acheson, "The President and the Secretary of State," p. 40. Interview with Paul H. Nitze, April 15, 1966.

[12] Interview with Dean Acheson, April 14, 1966.

as executive secretaries, might assume policy-making, not just administrative, functions.

Third, in interdepartmental meetings and committees, the Secretary of State must assume the leadership in policy discussions. The Secretary should encourage the exchange of ideas to be candid and frank, for the purpose of interdepartmental meetings is more than to reach a consensus on recommendations or policy papers. These meetings should represent opportunities to arrive at basic understandings. And where there are differences of opinion, they should be explored—not hidden. Basic conflicts on issues and wide divergencies of perspective should be referred to the President for final decision.

Fourth, the Secretary of State must encourage his subordinates within the Department to maintain close ties with their colleagues in other departments. Since foreign policy must be viewed in all its dimensions—economic, military, cultural, political—the Secretary of State and his subordinates benefit from "brain picking" experts in other departments. The more the State Department staff understands about the interaction of the multifarious aspects of foreign policy, the more sophisticated and comprehensive will be the policy suggestions that "bubble-up" from its depths.[13] Knowledge is power in the foreign-policy process, and better-educated policy suggestions will add authority to the State Department's coordinating position *vis-à-vis* other decisional and policy-making units. At the same time, its external orientation will please the other policy units that have been consulted on a regular and systematic basis.

Fifth, the Secretary of State must make a particularly strenuous effort to establish an intimate working relationship between himself and the Secretary of Defense. The Secretary of State must see that both he and his senior officers meet regularly with

[13] Acheson, "The Responsibility for Decision in Foreign Policy," p. 8.

the Secretary of Defense and the Joint Chiefs of Staff for thorough discussions of strategic policy. For, as Acheson has said, "foreign policy and military policy divorced from one another are both operating in the field of phantasy."[14] Acheson, of course, realizes that the type of relationship between the civilians and the military is determined to a large extent by the personalities who are in control of the high commands in each camp. Because a good relationship is indispensable to a coherent foreign policy, he believes the Secretary of State must make every effort to maintain friendly relations with the Secretary of Defense. If he fails, then the Secretary of State must take his case for smoother relations directly to the President. Essentially, a Secretary with a comprehensive knowledge of military strategy will be judged favorably by the professionals in the Defense Department and by the President.

Sixth, the Secretary of State must be an ardent supporter of the executive departments as the major channel through which the President receives his information. By accentuating the traditional importance of the executive departments, the Secretary of State can add to his own policy-making stature within the competitive environment of interdepartment interaction. On the positive side, he can emphasize the venerable place of the Secretary of State within the Cabinet. Acheson describes the return of General Marshall to the Truman Cabinet, this time as Secretary of Defense:

> When he returned to the Cabinet in 1950, it seemed natural to all of us that next to the President deference was due to General Marshall. But he would have none of it. The Secretary of State was the senior officer to whom he punctiliously deferred, not only in matters of protocol but in council as well.[15]

On the negative side, stress on his formal preeminency forestalls

[14] *Ibid.*, p. 11.
[15] Acheson, *Sketches from Life of Men I Have Known*, p. 165.

the President from relying too readily or too heavily upon special White House advisers, the executive secretaries of interdepartmental committees like the National Security Council, or personal friends of the "kitchen cabinet" type.

Seventh, Acheson is convinced that the Secretary of State must do all that he can to make certain that he participates in making all crisis decisions. This he can do by establishing himself as an idea man, by being physically available, and by entrenching himself as the official who coordinates foreign policies for the President. During times of recurring crises, the Secretary of State must more than ever demonstrate superior knowledge of the diverse facets of the foreign-policy process and prove to the President and his own peers that he can operate and coordinate these variables intelligently and authoritatively under stress. He then can expect that he will at least be assigned by the President to membership on crisis groups, and, more than likely, to the key coordinating position in these *ad hoc* units.[16]

The Secretary of State's positions as chief coordinator, foremost adviser, and constant participant in the foreign-policy process are all directly tied to his relationship to the President. He can, and must, work to improve the methods and procedures of inter-institutional coordination. He can, and must, struggle to retain his position in the foreign policy-making arena by perfecting his own personal abilities and insights. Yet the key to his success in the interpersonal and inter-institutional interaction aspects of the foreign-policy process unquestionably is found in his ability to win and retain the confidence and respect of his chief, the President of the United States.

[16] Snyder and Paige, "The United States Decision to Resist Aggression," pp. 223–224. From this study of the Korean decision, there is no doubt that this situation is a demonstration of how Acheson wants a President to use his Secretary of State in a crisis situation.

CHAPTER SIX

The Secretary of State and the Conduct of Foreign Policy in a Democracy

As observed earlier, Dean Acheson's relations with Congress and the press were often strained and antagonistic during his tenure as Secretary of State. Some commentators have suggested that Acheson's conception of democratic elements and their roles in the making of foreign policy were, and remain, cloudy and inconsistent.[1] It is a matter of record that he was brusque with Congressmen, hostile to the news media, and impatient with public opinion. Nevertheless, Acheson's perceptions of the foreign policy-making process in relation to the larger democratic process has exhibited, over the years, a consistent and coherent pattern.

[1] For example, Graebner, *An Uncertain Tradition: American Secretaries of State in the Twentieth Century,* pp. 286–287.

Acheson's operational code for the Secretary of State as a policy maker demands that the Secretary interact with the democratic aspects of the American political system in a specified fashion, to assure his power position in the policy-making process. The concepts of the struggle syndrome, the State Department's professionalism, and the special relationship between the President and the Secretary of State are interrelated with Acheson's perception of the Secretary's relationship to the public. Several generalized assumptions that control Acheson's perception of the democratic environment in the United States serve as parameters within which the Secretary of State must operate to maximize his effectiveness as a policy maker.

First, Acheson asserts that the democratic elements must be viewed in the context of the American political system. The Secretary must understand its traditions, precedents, and institutions so that he can effectively maneuver within the system in his efforts to achieve his policy goals. The political devices and institutions of one system should not be grafted on to another. For example, the "question hour" and the "cabinet concept," established features of the British parliamentary system, have no place in the American Presidential system. Proposed institutional, organizational, or political improvements must pass the test of compatibility with the Presidential system; otherwise, they are dangerous, pernicious abstractions.[2]

Second, only the President and the executive branch of the government can furnish the leadership necessary for consistency and coherency in United States foreign policy. Neither Congress nor any other institution or person can take the place of the President as the final architect of the foreign-policy process. The intellectual enterprise of making policy is a secluded one. The Secretary of

[2] Acheson, *A Citizen Looks at Congress,* pp. 79–80. Acheson seems to be opposed to any grand designs that purport to have the answers to the improvement needs of the American political system.

State must therefore ensure that creative efforts by State Department professionals at the early stages of policy formulation are shielded from large, public intrusions. This credo, Acheson has stated,

> ... leads to two suggestions: first, that policy should be formulated before it is announced; and, second, that there may be better ways than through legislation to announce policy. One has to do with substance; the other with method.[3]

Although public discussions of policy are indeed indispensable to a democratic political system, they should intrude only at the latter stages of policy determination.

The American democratic process operates on a base of conflict. There is constant struggle between the branches of government, between institutions, and between individuals. Power strikes power, and the Secretary of State is inextricably involved in a struggle arena. As a policy maker, he must cope with the pressures from Congress, the news media, and public opinion in such a fashion that they do not force him to enter into conflict on their terms or at their chosen levels of the policy-formulation process.

Acheson also firmly believes in the essential ability of democratic nations to remain energetic and viable actors in the international arena, today and in the future. Although the formulation of foreign policy in a democratic society contains some elements of difficulty not found in closed societies such as Russia and China, democratic societies have time on their side. As more and more people become aware of the close connection between domestic and foreign policies, the complexities and countinuing problems in international affairs, and the inability of the United

[3] Acheson, "Middle East Policy," p. 234.

States to solve or control all problems in all parts of the world, the prospects for eventual American success will increase.

From this foundation of interacting and interrelated factors, Acheson constructs the public interaction variable for the Secretary of State in his role as a policy maker. For the purposes of this study, the policy-making process is divided into seven steps: (1) precondition, (2) perception of the problem(s), (3) search for alternatives, (4) choice, (5) legitimation, (6) execution, and (7) feedback.[4] This, it is hoped, will help to identify approximately where Acheson feels it is appropriate for democratic elements to enter into the process. From this theoretical base, an analysis will be made of Acheson's interpretation of the interaction of the Secretary of State with Congress, public opinion, and the news media.

One of the major concerns of the Secretary of State in his relations with Congress is to demonstrate convincingly to the legislators that it is the executive that is the primary leadership branch in the area of foreign affairs. By staunchly defending the Presidential prerogative in foreign policy; by protecting his State Department colleagues against investigative abuses; and by presenting policies to Congress with authority and confidence, the Secretary of State reinforces his own position as well as that of the Chief Executive.

There is nothing static about the balance of power set up by the Constitution between the President and Congress, Acheson points out. The kinetic equilibrium resulting from the counterthrusts of strong forces is the bedrock of the American policy-making process, and must be so recognized by the Secretary of State. Within this struggle syndrome, he must guard the Executive

[4] For other processes in decision-making or policy making, see Lasswell, *The Decision Process;* Lerche and Said, *Concepts of International Politics,* pp. 30–44.

from any encroachment into the field of foreign-policy determination. Congress cannot create a foreign-policy program:

> [Congress] is not structurally organized to exert that leadership. Information necessarily comes to it periodically and predigested. It is not in continuous contact with foreign leaders. It is not in a position to assess on a day-to-day basis the opportunities and dangers which spring up in remote places and then relate them to a happening ten thousand miles away. The Congress, in short, is not, was not intended to be, and cannot be an Executive.[5]

On the one hand, the Secretary of State must stress Presidential leadership in the field of foreign affairs; on the other hand, it is his duty to present and sponsor before Congress the foreign-policy programs of the President. In dealing with Congress, Acheson offers several formulas for a Secretary of State to advance the Administration's proposals:

First, his meetings with congressional committees and subcommittees must not be allowed to degenerate into platforms from which Representatives browbeat the Secretary in hopes of channeling their influence into the executive policy-making arena. The Secretary must make sure that his trips to the "Hill" are beneficial for both parties concerned. Influence must be a two-way street—from the President to Congress, and from Congress back to the President, with the Secretary striving for meaningful interaction within the congressional committee system and the Chief Executive.

Second, the Secretary of State must be in a position to speak to Congressmen as an authoritative representative of the Administration. When he cannot tell the "whole" truth to Congress, he must at least tell nothing but the truth. Acheson scoffs at commentators who report that executive agents must "get along" with

[5] Acheson, *A Democrat Looks at His Party,* pp. 106–107.

Congress and particularly with the Senate. If this means that concessions of policy must be made in the interest of affability, then, says Acheson, congeniality must be rejected. It is the duty of the Secretary to be ready for battle with Congressmen when matters of principle are at stake: "[M]utual respect is more important than affability" in producing positive results in the legislative-executive policy-making arena.[6]

Third, the Secretary must be willing to devote both time and energy to congressional committees. For the committees, especially their chairmen, are seats of great power, and they must be made aware that the Secretary is an authoritative and candid spokesman for the Administration on foreign-policy matters. His influence may be extended into the congressional committee power centers by a number of techniques: cultivation of friendly relations with the committee chairmen; both formal and informal transmission to the chairmen of information on policies being developed in their areas; thorough preparation prior to appearing before committees—the Secretary must never attempt to bluff a committee; vigorous presentations in support of the Administration's programs; informal and frequent consultations with key congressional leaders before important changes in policy are proposed by the administration (e.g., NATO); and emphasis on the national security aspects of a policy when he tries to "sell" it to Congress, stressing its importance to national self-interests. As Acheson has said, ". . . the time spent in congressional meetings is spent—and, for the most part, well spent—in the performance of one of [the Secretary's] most important duties."[7]

Still, the Secretary of State must repel any congressional intrusions into the internal policy-making processes of his Department. Although the desire of Congressmen to know details of decision making in the Department may be natural, to indulge it would

[6] Acheson, *A Citizen Looks at Congress,* pp. 75–76.
[7] *Ibid.,* p. 65.

destroy the administrative process and organization. The Secretary must assume full responsibility for shielding his colleagues within the Department from the unequal struggle with a congressional investigation.

Fourth, the Secretary of State must acknowledge the growth in importance of the House of Representatives in the foreign-policy process. Leading members of the House, as well as those in the Senate, must be fully informed of policy proposals so that the House members will not squeeze the purse strings on important Administration foreign-policy programs.

Fifth, and last, the Secretary of State must face the fact that, since legislative–executive relations are basically political and vary greatly with particular circumstances, he himself becomes a political figure. As a close colleague of the President, he will be the target of much partisan criticism. Moreover, Acheson cautions, the Secretary of State, at times, "... is destined to be a pariah with Congress because he represents problems which the Congress wishes to forget. Votes can be lost but not gained through foreign policy."[8] Acheson insists that a Secretary of State must be a strong supporter of the President's foreign-policy program when he appears before Congress as the Administration's spokesman; he cannot, and must not, hedge on his commitments to the President and to the Administration's foreign-policy program. In the process, though, he is unavoidably caught "smack in the middle" of the game of politics, regardless of his desires.[9]

[8] Acheson, "The Responsibility for Decision in Foreign Policy," p. 9.

[9] Interview with Dean Acheson, April 14, 1966; Acheson, *A Citizen Looks at Congress,* pp. 33–34. In the light of this, Acheson personally is opposed to having strong, disciplined parties based on sharp ideological differences as contenders for power in the American political system. This, he says, would only tend to paralyze the development of any effective United States foreign policy when the President and Congress were of different parties. In addition, election results would throw to the winds the continuity and consistency needed in a foreign policy.

Throughout his writings, Acheson reiterates his belief that policy must be shielded from congressional intrusion in its early stages of formulation. Some key Senators and Congressmen may perhaps be brought into the process at fairly early stages; however, the policy itself must be formulated in the executive branch before it is proposed to Congress. The foreign-policy program must be consolidated in the hands of the foreign-policy professionals under the direction of the Secretary of State, with the final authority resting with the President. Most Congressmen cannot be fully enough informed to enter the policy process until the stage of legitimation. Nor is Congress structurally or emotionally prepared to formulate foreign policy. However, when the legitimation stage in policy formulation is reached, Acheson believes that Congress not only can but should enter the process. It must impose the penalty of scathing criticism upon the meretricious proposals and give support to good ones, and it must point out the way to think about, appraise and criticize policies. As Acheson describes the process, "the President initiates and formulates" foreign policies, while "the Congress modifies, approves, or vetoes."[10] The Secretary of State must relate to Congress in such a manner as to encourage Congress not to shirk these responsibilities. By participating in legitimation, Congress can do more than fulfill its obligation to analyze critically what has been formulated in the executive branch. It can also undertake to educate the American people to the ramifications of the policy proposed.

[10] Acheson, *A Citizen Looks at Congress,* pp. 117–119. At this point, it is necessary to mention that some political scientists disagree with Mr. Acheson's formula for congressional involvement in the foreign-polcy process. Some believe that Congress can and must take more of the initiative in the formulation of foreign policy; e.g. Dahl, *Congress and Foreign Policy,* and Robinson, *Congress and Foreign Policy-Making: A Study in Legislative Influence and Initiative.*

Acheson has remarked that foreign policy, instead of remaining the province of a few professionals, has become a personal question for each one of us. As more and more people become interested in foreign policy, the Secretary of State and his colleagues must seek to communicate to them the complexities and difficulties of the external realm. Nevertheless, the Secretary must maintain the right to inaugurate new policies and to bring them to maturity free from public scrutiny and pressure. It is the Secretary's task to shield evolving concepts from the public.

Acheson recognizes the dilemma for the Secretary of State in choosing between the great need for as full and quick public information as possible and the parallel need for privacy and calm in the first stages of policy formulation. When a policy's tentative direction has been determined, the public can be brought into the policy-making process. Even here, however, when the public is not clear in its acceptance of a particular policy, the President must exert leadership to implement a policy that he and his advisers deem essential to America's national security. A policy maker must try to feel the pulse of the people, yet he must do what he thinks is right and necessary in particular situations and hope that the people will retroactively support his policy directions. Acheson cites Truman's stance on the Korean war and Johnson's stance in relation to the Vietnam struggle as examples of policy making that has been done with the intention of doing what is best for American national security. And yet it is evident, says Acheson, that the people will not always respond positively after the fact; hence, the American people must be made aware of the critical nature of certain policy decisions.

The State Department must be close to the American people, constantly reporting facts without which informed judgments or criticism cannot be forthcoming. The Department must do its best to keep the American people advised so that when they are called upon to enter the policy-making process, they will be able to discuss and debate the alternatives with maturity, restraint, and candor.[11]

Acheson advises a Secretary of State and his State Department colleagues to educate the American citizen to four important precepts about international politcs: First, Americans must be taught to think realistically about foreign affairs. They must be made aware that the problems of international relations will be with them for a long time; they cannot be solved by abstract wishes to build a heaven on earth. The United States can hope to solve only some international issues, and these only through a slow step-by-step process. The American people must never be led to believe that peaceful ends in international relations can be reached by gadgets or through moral fervor, and without the pain of hard thinking, hard work, and some real risk and sacrifice.

Second, Americans must be reminded that there is no such phenomenon as complete security. The illusion of absolute security has caused Americans, time and again, to overestimate the power and influence of the United States in the international arena. Times change, situations change, and, therefore, the requirements of national security must be adjusted and readjusted in the light of the fluctuating environment of the international system.

Third, the American people must be alerted against demogogic oversimplifications, such as calls for scapegoats, absolutisms, and "morality." Emotional and disruptive outbursts by

[11] In his speeches and writings, Acheson devotes much attention to the importance of education as a factor in ensuring that policies will be discussed with restraint and maturity; Acheson, "United States Foreign Policy," p. 37: "But it is also the obligation of all of us who participate in these public discussions to speak responsibly and soberly in order that we will not unwittingly further the Soviet purpose of isolating us." Acheson, "Problems in American Foreign Policy," p. 669: "When people agree with us [the State Department] we want their support; when they do not, we want their frank and constructive criticism."

those who hunger after easy solutions to America's involvements in world affairs almost always prove detrimental to an administration's efforts to construct a consistent and coherent foreign-policy program. It is up to the Secretary of State to take the lead in making Americans aware of the complexities of constructing a foreign-policy program in a revolutionary world arena so that Americans can discuss and debate foreign policy issues in a constructive, mature, and restrained manner.

Fourth, the American people must be put on guard against "crisis builders" and propagandists who try to capitalize on the complexities and difficulties of foreign affairs to exploit personalities and institutions for their personal gain–political or financial. The public needs the sophistication to reject advertising gimmicks and propaganda techniques used by some news commentators and political agitators to fan crisis situations by distortion, oversimplification, and character vilification.[12]

It is not easy to conduct foreign policy in a democracy; however, the pressures from the democratic elements in an open society force a policy maker to ponder what he is doing and how he may best justify his actions. A strong democratic society protects against despotic, irresponsible decisions by national leaders.

Acheson's personal relations with the news media during the twelve years he was in the State Department were never happy. No doubt as a result, he believes that the Secretary of State should usually shield all except the latter policy-making steps from newsmen.

Acheson sees the roles of the Secretary of State and the news

[12] Acheson, "'Random Harvest': The Perverted Ingenuity of Propaganda," p. 634; see also some of Acheson's remarks made in relation to McCarthy and McCarthyism.

media to be in direct conflict when it comes to policy formulation. The Secretary must guard a policy in its embryonic stages against "leaks" or public discussion, so that its development into an operational policy suggestion will not be stunted. The news media, on the other hand, concerned with attitudes rather than consequences, seek news material regardless of the effects on policy. Hence, the Secretary of State must beware of reporters who want to know too much too early, of commentators who try to pressure policy makers into too-quick initiatives, and of public-opinion polls that are conducted on the basis of piecemeal information.

Acheson does not advocate that the Secretary of State either rebuff or ignore the press. What he does insist is that the Secretary retain his independence, that he not be swayed from the contemplation of long-range policy by the demands of newsmen with their daily, weekly, and monthly deadlines.[13] The Secretary must at all times be free and determined, whatever the publicity and propaganda enthusiasts may advise, to reject any and all proposals contrary to the nation's best interests.

The danger of open diplomacy, for example, is that instead of negotiations being forums where agreements can be made, they become sounding boards for propaganda statements. The Secretary must safeguard some aspects of traditional diplomacy so that he stands a chance of controlling the diplomatic variables in the search for compromise. He must not allow the press to manipulate him or the President into conferences which accomplish nothing but empty slogans. Only the Secretary of State can fight the abuses of open diplomacy:

[13] Acheson, *A Democrat Looks at His Party,* pp. 194–197; Acheson, "Europe: Decision or Drift," p. 198. Acheson says the Secretary of State must look at the "continuum of events," he must take a long-range view of decisions. He cannot satisfy himself with the rush for quick judgments in order to reach a publishing deadline.

No outsider has the information—though many commentators seem to think they have—or the control over the timing of action, or over the personnel through whom action is taken, to do this.[14]

One of the most difficult tasks of the Secretary of State is to educate the American people to the fact that there is no world conscience. Although public opinion is important to the American political system, it does not follow that the United States must "worry" about world public opinion. Americans must learn to exorcise image worship in the international arena; they must learn that the American image will take care of itself when the United States stresses actions and policies, rather than propaganda and slogans. "World opinion simply does not exist on the matters which concern us;" it is a "body of folklore," which must not be allowed to interfere with America's pursuit of its own interests.[15] To place too much concern on the mythical concept of world public opinion can only cause the United States to base its policies on abstractions, slogans, or inactions. Self-criticism in the context of world public opinion must be avoided:

> I think that we should be careful to see that our self-examination and self-criticism does not go to the point where it becomes self-reproach, because that attitude of mind is one which is apt to bring paralysis in the field of action where action is necessary. We must examine ourselves but we must not get into the state of merely reproaching ourselves . . .[16]

Though Acheson highlights the difficulties for the Secretary of State in his role as a policy maker in a democratic society, he is

[14] Acheson, *Power and Diplomacy,* pp. 71–72; see also Acheson, "Danger in 'Summit' Talks," p. 92.

[15] Acheson, "The American Image Will Take Care of Itself," pp. 25, 95.

[16] U.S. Department of State, *Strengthening the Forces of Freedom: Selected Speeches and Statements of Secretary of State Acheson, February 1949–April 1950* Washington, D.C.: U.S. Government Printing Office, 1950), p. 14.

confidently assured of the vitality of American society and its ability to go on meeting the challenges of the future. Only a society based on the free exchange of ideas and the dignity of the individual can provide leadership in the world of today—and tomorrow. It is Acheson's contention that:

> what we need is not less spirit of free inquiry, but more . . . free thought is the kernel of what we are defending, and it is also the strongest weapon in our arsenal. What is more, it is the principal binding force in our coalition.[17]

As long as the opinions expressed are constructive and restrained, Acheson believes that the cacophony of opinions expressed in the United States, even during times of crisis, is truly a sound of American strength.

Still, Acheson places his faith in a democratic society that is more interested in what it does than in what it says. Its success can only be assured by placing the conduct of American foreign policy in the hands of the professional doers—the President and the Secretary of State. Foreign policy can never be formulated and executed through exhortations, public-opinion polls, or psuedo-scientific abstractions. It must, instead, be based on strong leadership within the democratic process.

[17] Acheson, "The High Price of World Leadership," p. 9.

CHAPTER SEVEN

Conclusions

Alexander DeConde has constructed a generalized theory of an ideal Secretary of State:

> [A]n outstanding Secretary is one who has great ideas and principles, that is ideas that transcend immediate and local problems, one who has been given the power to participate in the making of important decisions and to mold his ideas into policy, and who has the diplomatic skill and statesmanship to carry out policy in international affairs. . . .
> At the same time, the outstanding Secretary is one who retains the overall direction of foreign policy against the parochial interests of other agencies dealing with foreign affairs. He is one who can establish and maintain his authority within his own department, in the Cabinet, and in his rela-

tions with the President. He is one who can keep those with independent political support, from inside his own department and without, from stepping between himself and the President. He is one who realizes that he can refine and enrich decisions, can persuade the President to take action, but does not have to be reminded that he does not himself possess the power of final decision. He is one who is jealous of his prestige and that of his office, for he understands that such prestige is an important tool in carrying out foreign policy. . . . Finally, the truly great Secretary of State will give style and cohesion to foreign policy as a whole . . . the outstanding Secretary will always realize also that no one part of his duties, or his office, can be wholly isolated from the other parts, that all belong to an interacting whole.[1]

The Acheson policy-making code, as developed throughout this book, systematically builds an operationalized framework that identifies and analyzes those techniques and procedures Acheson believes a Secretary of State must master in order to maximize his position in the policy-making process.

The undergirding for the operational code analyzed above can most acurately be described as a partnership pattern fundamentally based upon a junior-senior hierarchical relationship between the President and the Secretary of State. The informal aspects of the relationship may be as important, if not more so, than the formal. However, under no circumstance does Acheson allow for the basic hierarchical, constitutional relationship to be violated. This is not to imply that Acheson discovered the partnership pattern of Presidential–Secretary of State relationships; rather, it is to accentuate the fact that Acheson was the key personality to operationalize this pattern in the transitional post-World War II period of America's increased and new involvements in world affairs.

[1] DeConde, *The American Secretary of State*, pp. 170–171.

Other types of patterns of relationships have of course existed between the President and the Secretary of State. They will be categorized below, and contrasted with the Acheson partnership pattern. In addition, other scholars might, in the future, want to analyze other actors in the office of the Secretary of State to identify and study the multidimensional aspects of these types so that an operationalized framework may be added to each of the idealized relationship patterns discussed below.

First, there is the ideal-type relationship in which the Secretary of State functions mainly as a "clerk." Here the President chooses to be his own Foreign Minister. For his Secretary, he wants no more than a man with administrative abilities sufficient to direct and coordinate the vast structure of the State Department. The Acheson pattern is at odds with this narrow managerial assignment, since it obviously deprives the Secretary of an active policy-making role.

Second, there is the ideal-type in which the Secretary of State serves as a figurehead. Again, in this situation the President chooses to be his own Secretary of State. However, here the Secretary of State does perform one important policy-making function. Either because of his popularity with the public or with Congress, he is used by the President to gain support for the Administration's foreign-policy programs. Otherwise, the Secretary's position is strictly symbolic. He does not even control his own Department; many times the President deals directly with his subordinates, for whom the President has more respect as foreign-policy professionals. Acheson rejects this type too, since he perceives the Secretary of State to be the final and authoritative leader of the State Department.

Third, there is the ideal-type in which the Secretary of State assumes the role of the President's Prime Minister. Based on his belief that his knowledge of international affairs is greater than the President's, the Secretary becomes the chief formulator of foreign policies; he presumes that he knows more about international affairs than does the President. Acheson categorically rejects this pattern for several reasons: it is constitutionally illegal; it is politically dangerous; and it is confusing to allies and enemies alike not to be able to identify the final spokesman for American foreign policy.

Even more important than contrasting the Acheson pattern of the President–Secretary of State relationship with other idealized types, is the abstraction of major generalizations from the Acheson operational code and their application to the policy-making role of the Secretaries of State of today and tomorrow.

James V. Forrestal, the first Secretary of Defense under Truman, wrote:

> The difficulty of government work . . . is that such work not only has to be done well, but the public has to be convinced that it is being well done. In other words, there is a necessity both for competence and exposition, and I hold it is extremely difficult to combine the two in the same person.[2]

Both Acheson's long-range perceptions and his service as Secretary of State confirm the mutual importance of competence and exposition. The stage at which the Secretary thinks the public should enter the policy-making process may vary with the personality of the Secretary and with the nature of the policy; but at some point it is incumbent that the people be persuaded to support the Administration's program.

Acheson highlights a universal phenomenon that all postwar Secretaries of State have had to accept, whether they want to or not—that is, that every Secretary finds himself unavoidably embroiled in the field of politics. Acheson's operational code accentuates three major factors that have exacerbated the Secretary's position in the partisan political battles in the American govern-

[2] Millis, ed., *The Forrestal Diaries,* p. 300.

ment: (1) There has developed a consciousness in the American electorate of the tight interlocking between the domestic and foreign policies of the United States. (2) The Secretary of State's intimate identification with the President makes him an ideal target for indirect political attacks on the President. (3) The public has become more aware of the United States' involvement in world affairs and of those officials assigned the duty of making American foreign policy. The Secretary of State has thus emerged as a conspicuous figure in an area that has become a legitimate battleground for spirited political debate. As James Forrestal expressed it:

> I have always been amused by those who say that they are quite willing to go into government, but they are not willing to go into politics. My answer, which has now become a bromide with me, is that you can no more divorce government from politics than you can separate sex from creation.[3]

The Acheson operational code confirms the premise that most policies and decisions in the foreign-policy process are made either on the basis of unsatisfactory information (either too much or too little) or in crisis situations. The revolutionary world environment of increased American involvement and technological advancements has accentuated the rapid fluctuations in the international system. Time and again, Acheson reports, the Secretary of State must make decisions to cope with the problems of the world on a step-by-step basis. The Secretary must never try to formulate policies based on wishful thinking or optimal solutions, such as making the world forever safe for democracy. Every Secretary of State must seek workable solutions to immediate problems and situations, while retaining a long-range strategic outlook for American interests. In other words, the Acheson code demonstrates the fact that most decisions in the foreign-

[3] *Ibid.*, p. 495.

policy process, by necessity, have to be less than optimal decisions.[4]

The Secretary of State must also be alert to the constant changes within the policy-making process itself. There is automatic and reciprocal feedback between the internal, national-policy process and the external, international environment; solution of a problem in either necessarily gives birth to new problems. The Secretary of State must always take account of the transformations occurring within the international system so that he can adapt procedures and policies to reinforce both his personal leadership within the internal foreign-policy process and the United States' leadership in the international political process.

Internal foreign-policy making is also closely linked to its execution. Acheson leaves no doubt that in spite of differences of administrative styles among Secretaries of State, a Secretary of State must convince the President one way or another that the State Department will implement a Presidential decision with precision and dispatch. This can only be done by direct supervision of the administration of his department by the Secretary himself. The Secretary's less tangible power bases, such as personal competence and intimate friendships, gain an institutional foundation through demonstrated ability of the State Department to make a verbal policy operational in an efficient manner.

Regardless of how a Secretary of State chooses to phrase it, he has to "fight like hell" to retain a position of primacy in the foreign-policy process against "kitchen cabinet" advisers, the traditional departments, new institutions, and suggested reorgan-

[4] March and Simon, *Organizations,* p. 209. To express it more generally, one may quote from March and Simon, and say that most of the Secretary's policy recommendations are based on the concept of satisfying:

> "Most human decision-making, whether individual or organizational, is concerned with the discovery and selection of satisfactory alternatives; only in exceptional cases is it concerned with the discovery and selection of optimal alternatives."

izations. Such phenomena as institutional proliferation, the expansion of the Defense Department, the increasing importance of the Secretary of Defense, the structured interdepartmental policy-making committees (NSC), the growth of the "invisible government" agencies (CIA), and the suggestions for a new Super-Secretary of Foreign Affairs, all threaten a Secretary of State's role as the President's foremost adviser on foreign-policy problems. Some Secretaries may use techniques different from those prescribed within the Acheson operational code, but the general proposition that struggle and competition are inherent in the job cannot be denied. Each Secretary of State will in his own way have to resist intrusions in old and new forms that imperil his policy-making authority.

Among all the generalizations to be drawn from this investigation, none is more clearly and universally important to the role of the Secretary of State than the variable of personality. Personality is the intangible thread that holds together all the other more visible elements of a Secretary of State's power base. The personal relationship between the President and the Secretary is, to Acheson, a dynamic variable which not only must be adjusted anew with each new combination of men, but also readjusted from time to time by long-term associates in the two offices. As Christian Herter, former Secretary of State under President Eisenhower, has written:

> The relationship between the President and the Secretary of State is, of necessity, a very personal one. Over the years, it has varied with circumstance and personalities and will undoubtedly continue to do so. The relationship can never be considered fixed . . . and any effort to make it so would hamper rather than enhance effective performance.[5]

[5] Christian A. Herter, "The Secretary of State," *The National Security Council,* ed. Henry M. Jackson (New York: Frederick A. Praeger, Inc., 1965), p. 141.

In addition to its emphasis on the Secretary's personal relations with the President, Acheson's operational code also affirms a generalization widely accepted by public administrators since the end of the Second World War, that there is an active interplay between the individual personality and the institutional organization of which he is a part. Acheson more particularly suggests that there can be no dichotomy between the Secretary of State and his Department. In other words, the personality of the Secretary of State will influence the institutional personality of the State Department—and, as Acheson discovered in the "Hiss affair," it has become extremely difficult for any Secretary of State to separate his private, individual personality from his public, institutional personality.

The Acheson code forcefully suggests that the philosophical perceptions of a Secretary of State on life, politics, and international relations determine to a large degree how he will perceive his personal policy-making role, as well as the collective role of the United States in world affairs. There will, therefore, be a mixture of objective facts, subjective values, and personal motivations in the policy suggestions that are presented to a President by a Secretary of State. In short, as Arnold Rogow has implied in his study of James Forrestal, it is difficult to avoid the conclusion that in most policy makers, personality needs and policy recommendations are closely related.

Nevertheless, Acheson implies, and the operational code developed above confirms, that the Secretary of State makes his most indelible mark upon the policy-making process by the policies that become identified with him and with the Administration in which he serves.[6] Personalities and organizations change so rapidly that the Secretary has only a transient impact upon the

[6] This point was confirmed by nearly every key personality who was interviewed by the author.

State Department's influence and organization. New personalities and new organizational groupings tend to arise as each new President–Secretary of State combination appears on the scene, but history remembers the policies of Secretaries of State and their Chief Executives. Hence, a Secretary can most help the position of future Secretaries of State by actively promoting the formulation, adoption, and efficient execution of foreign policies that he perceives to be in the American interest.

Acheson indicates that the Secretary of State faces, and will continue to face, a difficult policy-making role as a result of indigenous conflicts within the office itself. The Secretary occupies a position of dilemmas. He must walk the thin line between antagonistic political elements: he must fulfill his duty as institutional leader of the State Department while maintaining the closest personal relationship with the President. He must have the support of the Congress, yet he must protect his subordinates from too much Congressional interference. The office of the Secretary of State is obviously no sinecure.

The Acheson operational code has certain heuristic, authoritative, and behavioral dimensions that are important to the examination and understanding of the policy-making process and the Secretary of State's role in it. For example: (1) It is heuristic because it offers as an essential the contention that social scientists can better understand policy making if they investigate the process from the perspective of the actors themselves. (2) The Acheson code is authoritative, in that he has been recognized overwhelmingly as one of the most successful and influential Secretaries of State in American history. How he was able to achieve such a high level of success and influence is certainly determined to a large extent by how he perceived the policy-making role of the Secretary of State. (3) The code is also behavioral, because the conceptualization demonstrates and articulates the importance to the understanding of the policy-making process of such informal factors as personal friendships, personality motivations, and individual competence. In effect, informal bases of power may be more important than formal hierarchical positions in determining a person's influence in the policy-making process.

However, certain methodological and scientific limitations of the operational code as a research instrument in the social sciences do emerge. Whenever the factor of personality is interjected into an investigation in political science, whether it be decision-making models, totalitarian models, case studies, or operational codes, there is always the problem of uniqueness, self-justification, or misunderstood motives that can limit the adaptability of the framework to other political situations. Therefore, since times, personalities, and situations do change in the policy-making environment, there may be some question as to the adaptability of the Acheson code to other Secretaries of State. This, however, does not negate either the generalizations made above or the heuristic quality of this approach. Surely, a different personality may choose to accent different aspects of the position than Acheson recommends; still the fact remains that any Secretary of State must manipulate the variables analyzed above into an interacting, coordinated whole if he is to maximize the policy-making potentials of his office. That a different personality may choose to alter the variables within the environment to suit his own operating style does not obviate either the importance of the code itself as an example of the post-World War II partnership pattern or the universality of the variables regardless of what type of operating pattern a Secretary chooses (or is forced) to follow.[7]

The fact that this operational code is structured from the per-

[7] Neither do any of these limiting factors necessarily mean that the partnership pattern is not the "most functional" approach to the Secretary's role in the policy-making process.

ceptions of a particular personality may raise some questions about the generalizations that have been abstracted from it. However, when one relates the generalizations drawn from this specific, observer-participant conceptualization to those of broader historical–social science investigations into the role of the Secretary of State in the foreign-policy process, a high degree of correlation emerges. For "while different role incumbents are likely to differ in the way in which they interpret the requirements of their roles, the broad outlines of the role behavior will be similar regardless of the individual characteristics of the decision-maker."[8]

What appears to be needed in the discipline of political science is a "cluster" of investigations into the policy-making process constructed from the viewpoint of the actors themselves. In this way, a comparative analysis could be undertaken so that generalizations from a more representative base could be formulated. The regularity and consistency of the variables identified in each study would give more credence to the generalizations noted in this conclusion. In addition, the ideal-types identified above would be given more tangible meaning; and they could help either to substantiate or disapprove the generalizations made on the Secretary of State as a policy maker in the more historical, biographical, and journalistic writings.

In sum, recognizing the persistent difficulty of the social scientist—"breadth versus depth, generalization versus the bases (number of instances) on which generalization rests"[9]—the Acheson operational code was developed on the assumption that the

[8] Herbert C. Kelman, "Social-Psychological Approaches to the Study of International Relations: The Question of Relevance," *International Behavior: A Social-Psychological Analysis,* ed. Herbert C. Kelman (New York: Holt, Rinehart, and Winston, Inc., 1965), p. 588.

[9] Snyder and Paige, "The United States Decision to Resist Aggression," p. 228.

greater the depth of analysis into the office of the Secretary of State, the easier it would be to magnify and isolate those factors important to a Secretary's success. This approach was also favored because of the author's belief that there is a need for American political scientists to try to discover new methods and new techniques for explaining and analyzing the realities of political life. By focusing on a specific and conspicuous actor in the policy-making process, the technique of the operational code was used in an attempt to systematically blend the theoretical tools of the political scientist with the practical experiences of the operating official to achieve a fuller understanding of the policy-making process.

Bibliography

PUBLIC DOCUMENTS

Acheson, Dean G. *American Policy Toward China: Statement Before a Joint Senate Committee, June 4, 1951*. Washington, D.C.: United States Government Printing Office, 1951.

———. *Crisis in Asia—An Examination of U.S. Policy*. Washington, D.C.: United States Government Printing Office, 1950.

———. *Our Far Eastern Policy: Debate, Decision, and Action*. Washington, D.C.: United States Government Printing Office, 1951.

United States Department of State. *Guide to the U.N. in Korea*. Washington, D.C.: United States Government Printing Office, 1951.

———. *Our Foreign Policy 1952*. Washington, D.C.: United States Government Printing Office, 1952.

———. *Strengthening the Forces of Freedom: Selected Speeches and Statements of Secretary of State Acheson, February 1949–April 1950*. Washington, D.C.: United States Government Printing Office, 1950.

———. *The Joint Defense of Western Europe*. Washington, D.C.: United States Government Printing Office, 1951.

———. *Transcript of Roundtable Discussion on American Policy Toward China Held in the Department of State, October 6, 7, and 8, 1949*. Washington, D.C.: United States Printing Office, 1949.

United States Senate. 82nd Congress, 1st Session. Committee on Armed Services and the Committee on Foreign Relations. *Military Situation in the Far East: Part III*. Washington, D.C.: United States Government Printing Office, 1951.

———. 81st Congress, 1st Session. Committee on Foreign Relations. *Nomination of Dean G. Acheson, January 13, 1949*. Washington, D.C.: United States Government Printing Office, 1949.

———. 87th Congress, 1st Session. *Organizing for National Security: The Secretary of State and the National Security Policy Process*. Washington, D.C.: United States Government Printing Office, 1961.

———. 88th Congress, 1st Session. Subcommittee on National Security Staffing and Operations. *The Ambassador and the Problem of Coordination*. Washington, D.C.: United States Government Printing Office, 1963.

———. 86th Congress, 2nd Session. *The Role of the State Department in Coordinating the Reciprocal Trade Agreements Program*. Washington, D.C.: United States Government Printing Office, 1960.

BOOKS

Acheson, Dean G. *A Citizen Looks at Congress*. New York: Harper & Brothers, 1957.

———. *A Democrat Looks at His Party*. New York: Harper & Brothers, 1955.

———. *Morning and Noon*. Boston: Houghton Mifflin Company, 1965.

———. *Power and Diplomacy*. Cambridge, Massachusetts: Harvard University Press, 1958.

———. *Sketches from Life of Men I Have Known*. New York: Harper & Brothers, 1961.

Almond, Gabriel A. *The American People and Foreign Policy*. New York: Frederick A. Praeger, Inc., 1960.

Alperovitz, Gar. *Atomic Diplomacy: Hiroshima and Potsdam*. New York: Vintage Books, 1967.

Barnes, William, and Morgan, John Heath. *The Foreign Service of the United States*. Washington, D.C.: The Department of State, 1961.

Beal, John Robinson. *John Foster Dulles: A Biography*. New York: Harper & Brothers, 1957.

Beloff, Max. *The United States and the Unity of Europe*. Washington, D.C.: The Brookings Institution, 1963.

Bowie, Robert R. *Shaping the Future*. New York: Columbia University Press, 1964.

Brzezinski, Zbigniew, and Huntington, Samuel P. *Political Power: USA/USSR*. New York: The Viking Press, Inc., 1964.

Bundy, McGeorge, ed. *The Pattern of Responsibility*. Cambridge, Massachusetts: The Riverside Press, 1951.

Byrnes, James F. *All in One Lifetime*. New York: Harper & Brothers, 1958.

Cater, Douglass. *Power in Washington*. New York: Random House, Inc., 1964.

Cheever, Daniel S., and Haviland, H. Field, Jr. *American Foreign Policy and the Separation of Powers*. Cambridge, Massachusetts: Harvard University Press, 1952.

Dahl, Robert A. *Congress and Foreign Policy*. New York: Harcourt, Brace & World, Inc., 1950.

———. *Modern Political Analysis.* Englewood Cliffs, New Jersey: Prentice-Hall, Inc., 1963.

DeConde, Alexander. *The American Secretary of State: An Interpretation.* New York: Frederick A. Praeger, Inc., 1962.

Elder, Robert Ellsworth. *The Policy Machine.* Syracuse, New York: Syracuse University Press, 1960.

Eulau, Heinz. *The Behavioral Persuasion in Politics.* New York: Random House, Inc., 1963.

Gelber, Lionel. *America in Britain's Place.* New York: Frederick A. Praeger, Inc., 1961.

Goldman, Eric F. *The Crucial Decade—and After: America, 1945–1960.* New York: Vintage Books, 1960.

Graebner, Norman A. *Cold War Diplomacy: American Foreign Policy, 1945–1960.* Princeton, New Jersey: D. Van Nostrand Company, Inc., 1962.

———, ed. *An Uncertain Tradition: American Secretaries of State in the Twentieth Century.* New York: McGraw-Hill Book Company, Inc., 1961.

Hammond, Paul Y. *Organizing for Defense.* Princeton, New Jersey: Princeton University Press, 1961.

Hillman, William. *Mr. President.* New York: Farrar, Straus, and Young, Inc., 1952.

Huntington, Samuel P. *The Common Defense.* New York: Columbia University Press, 1961.

Jackson, Henry M., ed. *The National Security Council.* New York: Frederick A. Praeger, Inc., 1965.

———, ed. *The Secretary of State and the Ambassador.* New York: Frederick A. Praeger, Inc., 1964.

Johnson, E. A. J., ed. *The Dimensions of Diplomacy.* Baltimore, Maryland: The Johns Hopkins Press, 1964.

Jones, Joseph M. *The Fifteen Weeks.* New York: The Viking Press, Inc., 1955.

Kaufmann, William M. *The McNamara Strategy.* New York: Harper & Row, Inc., 1964.

Kelman, Herbert C., ed. *International Behavior: A Social-*

Psychological Analysis. New York: Holt, Rinehart, and Winston, Inc., 1965.

Koenig, Louis W., ed. *The Truman Administration: Its Principles and Practices*. New York: New York University Press, 1956.

Lasswell, Harold D. *The Decision Process*. College Park, Maryland: University of Maryland Press, 1956.

Lerche, Charles O., Jr., and Said, Abdul A. *Concepts of International Politics*. Englewood Cliffs, New Jersey: Prentice-Hall, Inc., 1963.

March, James G., and Simon, Herbert A. *Organizations*. New York: John Wiley & Sons, Inc., 1958.

Marx, Fritz Morstein, ed. *Elements of Public Administration*. Englewood Cliffs, New Jersey: Prentice-Hall, Inc., 1959.

Millis, Walter, ed. *The Forrestal Diaries*. New York: The Viking Press., Inc., 1951.

———. Mansfield, Harvey C., and Stein, Harold. *Arms and the State*. New York: The Twentieth Century Fund, Inc., 1958.

McCamy, James L. *Conduct of the New Diplomacy*. New York, Evanston, and London: Harper & Row, Inc., 1964.

McClelland, Charles A. *Theory and the International System*. New York: The Macmillan Company, 1966.

McLellan, David S. *The Cold War in Transition*. New York: The Macmilan Company, 1966.

Neustadt, Richard E. *Presidential Power, the Politics of Leadership*. New York: John Wiley & Sons, Inc., 1960.

Popper, Karl R. *The Open Society and Its Enemies*. Volume I. New York: Harper & Row, Inc., 1963.

Price, Don K., ed. *The Secretary of State*. Englewood Cliffs, New Jersey: Prentice-Hall, Inc., 1960.

Robinson, James A. *Congress and Foreign Policy-Making: A Study in Legislative Influence and Initiative*. Homewood, Illinois: Dorsey Press, 1962.

Rogow, Arnold A. *James Forrestal: A Study of Personality, Politics, and Policy*. New York: The Macmillan Company, 1963.

Rosenau, James N. *Public Opinion and Foreign Policy*. New York: Random House, Inc., 1961.

Rovere, Richard H. *Senator Joe McCarthy*. Cleveland and New York: Meridian Books, 1960.

Schlesinger, Arthur M., Jr. *A Thousand Days*. New York: A Fawcett Crest Book, 1965.

Shulman, Marshall D. *Stalin's Foreign Policy Reappraised*. Cambridge, Massachusetts: Harvard University Press, 1963.

Singer, J. David, ed. *Human Behavior and International Politics*. Chicago: Rand McNally & Company, 1965.

Sorauf, Francis J. *Political Science: An Informal Overview*. Columbus, Ohio: Charles E. Merrill Books, Inc., 1965.

Truman, Harry S. *Memoirs: Year of Decisions*. Volume I. Garden City, New York: Doubleday & Company, Inc., 1955.

———. *Memoirs: Years of Trial and Hope*. Volume II. Garden City, New York: Doubleday & Company, Inc., 1956.

Wohlstetter, Roberta. *Pearl Harbor: Warning and Decision*. Stanford, California: Stanford University Press, 1962.

Wolfenstein, E. Victor. *Personality and Politics*. Belmont, California: Dickenson Publishing Company, Inc., 1969.

ARTICLES AND PERIODICALS

Acheson, Dean G. "Adenauer and McCloy: Godfathers of the New Germany," *Harper's,* 222, No. 1331 (April, 1961), 40–45.

———. "Advice to Young Academic Propagandists," *The Reporter,* 33, No. 3 (August 12, 1965), 30.

———. "American-Soviet Friendship," *Vital Speeches,* 12, No. 4 (December 1, 1945), 110–112.

———. "Crisis in Asia—An Examination of U.S. Policy," *The Department of State Bulletin,* 22, No. 551 (January 23, 1950), 111–118.

———. "Danger in 'Summit' Talks," *U.S. News and World Report,* 44, No. 4 (April 25, 1958), 88–92.

———. "Danger in the World—and What to Do About It," *U.S. News & World Report,* 48, No. 24 (June 13, 1960), 116–119.

———. "Ernest Bevin: Comfortable Friend, Formidable Adversary," *Harper's,* 222, No. 1332 (May, 1961), 55–62.

———. "Ethics in International Relations Today," *Vital Speeches,* 31, No. 8 (February 1, 1965), 226–228.

———. "Europe: Decision or Drift," "*Foreign Affairs,* 44, No. 2 (January, 1966), 198–205.

———. "Facing Up to the Challenge of the Present World Crisis," *The Department of State Bulletin,* 24, No. 601 (January 8, 1951), 56.

———. "Fifty Years After," *The Yale Review,* 51, No. 1 (October, 1961), 1–10.

———. "Foreign Policy and Presidential Moralism," *The Reporter,* 16, No. 9 (May 2, 1957), 10–14.

———. "Foreign Policy Tradition of the United States," *Vital Speeches,* 13, No. 18 (July 1, 1947), 550–553.

———. "Fulfillment of Responsibility in a World in Peril," *The Department of State Bulletin,* 23, No. 589 (October 16, 1950), 613–616.

———. "Homage to General Marshall," *The Reporter,* 21, No. 9 (November 26, 1959), 25–28.

———. "How Are We Doing?" *Vital Speeches,* 18, No. 7 (January 15, 1952), 194–197.

———. "I Don't Share the Sense of Panic," *U.S. News & World Report,* 42, No. 3 (January 18, 1957), 126–131.

———. " 'Instant Retaliation': Debate Continued," *The New York Times Magazine* (March 28, 1954), 13, 77–78.

———. "Isolationists Are Stupid," *The Saturday Evening Post,* 238, 15 (July 31, 1965), 12–15.

———. "Journey into Our Times," *American Heritage,* 11, No. 2 (February, 1960), 44–47, 79.

———. "Korea in Perspective," *The Department of State Bulletin,* 23, No. 578 (July 31, 1950), 171–172.

———. "Legislative-Executive Relations," *The Yale Review,* 45, No. 4 (June, 1956), 481–495.

———. "Middle East Policy," *Vital Speeches,* 23, No. 8 (February 1, 1957), 234–238.

———. "Mr. Acheson on Ending the War: They Don't Negotiate a Stop," *The National Observer* (December 11, 1967), 4.

———. "Morality, Moralism, and Diplomacy," *The Yale Review,* 45, No. 4 (June, 1958), 481–493.

———. "Negotiation Is Only a Polite Phrase for a Retreat," *U.S. News & World Report,* 47, No. 22 (November 30, 1959), 110–111.

———. "North Atlantic Pact Proceedings," *The Department of State Bulletin,* 20, No. 504 (February 27, 1949), 263.

———. "On Dealing with Russia: An Inside View," *The New York Times Magazine* (April 12, 1958), 27, 88–89.

———. "Our Atlantic Alliance," *Vital Speeches,* 29, No. 6 (January 1, 1963), 162–166.

———. "Peace Through Strength: A Foreign Policy Objective," *The Department of State Bulletin,* 22, No. 573 (June 26, 1950), 1037–1041, 1056.

———. "Prelude to Independence," *The Yale Review,* 48, No. 4 (June, 1959), 481–490.

———. "Problems in American Foreign Policy," *The Department of State Bulletin,* 21, No. 539 (October 31, 1949), 668–669.

———. " 'Random Harvest': The Perverted Ingenuity of Propaganda," *Vital Speeches,* 12, No. 20 (August 1, 1946), 633–635.

———. "Review of *Shaping the Future: Foreign Policy in an Age of Transition* by Robert Bowie," *Political Science Quarterly,* 79, No. 3 (September, 1964), 435–436.

———. "The American Image Will Take Care of Itself," *The New York Times Magazine* (February 28, 1965), 24–25, 95.

———. "The Bases of a Foreign Program," *The New York Times Magazine* (January 6, 1957), 11, 32–34.

———. "The 'Debate' on Defense," *The Reporter,* 22, No. 5 (March 3, 1960), 27–28.
———. "The High Price of World Leadership," *The New Republic,* 129, 12 (October 19, 1953), 7–9.
———. "The Illusion of Disengagement," *Foreign Affairs,* 36, No. 3 (April, 1958), 371–382.
———. "The Parties and Foreign Policy," *Harper's,* 211, No. 1266 (November, 1955), 29–34.
———. "The Peace the World Wants," *The Department of State Bulletin,* 23, No. 587 (October 2, 1950), 523–529.
———. "The Practice of Partnership," *Foreign Affairs,* 41, No. 2 (January, 1963), 247–260.
———. "The Premises of American Policy," Editors, Walter R. Hahn and John C. Neff, *American Strategy for the Nuclear Age* (New York: Anchor Books, Doubleday & Company, Inc., 1960), 409–421.
———. "The Preservation of Peace," *Vital Speeches,* 15, No. 9 (February 15, 1949), 259–261.
———. "The President and the Secretary of State," John C. Price, ed., *The Secretary of State* (Englewood Cliffs, New Jersey: Prentice-Hall, Inc., 1960), 27–50.
———. "The Quality of American Patriotism," *The Department of State Bulletin,* 22, No. 565 (May 1, 1950), 696–698.
———. "The Responsibility for Decision in Foreign Policy," *The Yale Review,* 44, No. 1 (September, 1954), 1–12.
———. "Thoughts About Thought in High Places," United States Senate, *Organizing for National Security,* Volume II (Washington, D.C.: United States Government Printing Office, 1961), 290–298.
———. "Threats to Democracy and Its Way of Life," *The Department of State Bulletin,* 22, No. 565 (May 1, 1950), 673–677.
———. "To Meet the Shifting Soviet Offensive," *The New York Times Magazine* (April 15, 1956), 11, 69–78.
———. "United States Foreign Policy," Frederick Ungar, ed.,

What's Right With America (New York: Frederick Ungar Publishing Company, 1952), 27–38.
———. "What a Secretary of State Really Does," *Harper's,* 209, No. 1255 (December, 1954), 48.
———. "Wishing Won't Hold Berlin," *The Saturday Evening Post,* 231, No. 36 (March 7, 1959), 32, 85–86.
———. "Withdrawal from Europe? 'An Illusion'," *The New York Times Magazine* (December 15, 1963), 7, 67–69.
"Acheson on McCarthy," *The New Republic,* 122, No. 18 (May 1, 1950), 6.
"Acheson Sees Ike's Foreign Policy as 'Bluster and Bluff'," *U.S. News & World Report,* 41, No. 14 (October 5, 1956), 88–91.
"Acheson vs. Dulles on Foreign Policy," *U.S. News & World Report,* 40, No. 4 (January 27, 1956), 31–32.
Bagdikian, Ben H. "The 'Inner, Inner Circle' Around Johnson," *The New York Times Magazine* (February 28, 1965), 21, 78–84.
Falk, Stanley L. "The National Security Council Under Truman, Eisenhower, and Kennedy," *Political Science Quarterly,* 79, No. 3 (September, 1964), 403–434.
"Foreign Policies Toward Asia: A Television Interview with Secretary Acheson," *The Department of State Bulletin,* 23, No. 585 (September 18, 1950), 460–464.
Hamburger, Philip. "Profiles: Mr. Secretary, I," *The New Yorker,* 25, No. 38 (November 12, 1949), 39–53.
———. "Profiles: Mr. Secretary, II," *The New Yorker,* 25, No. 39 (November 19, 1949), 40–61.
"Misunderstood Men," *Harper's,* 211, No. 1266 (November, 1955), 18–20.
Nitze, Paul H. " 'Impossible' Job of Secretary of State," *The New York Times Magazine* (February 24, 1957), 60–61.
Reston, James. "Secretary Acheson: A First-Year Audit," *The New York Times Magazine* (February 22, 1950), 7–9, 35–38.
Richardson, Dow. "Open Letter to John Bartlett," *The Saturday Review,* 40, No. 12 (March 23, 1957), 32–34.

Rodell, Fred. "The Impeccable Mr. Acheson," *The American Mercury,* 70, No. 316 (April, 1950), 387–397.

Rusk, Dean. "The President," *Foreign Affairs,* 38, No. 3 (April, 1960), 353–369.

"Satisfactory Answers," *Time,* 53, No. 4 (January 24, 1949), 15.

Seabury, Paul. "The Establishment Game: Nicholas Murray Butler Rides Again," *The Reporter,* 34, No. 10 (May 19, 1966), 24–26.

"Secretary Acheson," *Fortune,* 30, No. 1 (April, 1949), 94–97.

"Secretary Acheson Explains Statement on Alger Hiss," *The Department of State Bulletin,* 22, No. 558 (March 13, 1950), 412–413.

"Secretary Acheson's Farewell to His Colleagues," *The Department of State Bulletin,* 28, No. 709 (January 26, 1953), 161–162.

Snyder, Richard C., and Paige, Glenn D. "The United States Decision to Resist Aggression in Korea: The Application of an Analytical Scheme," Editors, Richard C. Snyder, H. W. Bruck, and Burton Sapin, *Foreign Policy Decision-Making* (New York: The Free Press of Glencoe, 1962), 206–249.

Tucker, Robert C. "The Dictator and Totalitarianism," *World Politics,* 17, No. 4 (July, 1965), 555–583.

"U.S. Leadership: At Peak Under Truman?" *U.S. News & World Report,* 58, No. 17 (April 26, 1965), 30.

Warner, Albert L. "How the Korea Decision Was Made," *Harper's,* 202, No. 1213 (June, 1951), 99–106.

Wittmer, Felix. "Freedom's Case Against Dean Acheson," *The American Mercury,* 74, No. 340 (April, 1952), 3–17.

PAMPHLETS AND REPORTS

Hart, Hornell. *McCarthy Versus the State Department*. Durham, North Carolina: Duke University, 1952.

Pruitt, Dean G. *Problem Solving in the Department of State.* Denver, Colorado: University of Denver, 1965.

Report of the Committee on Foreign Affairs Personnel. *Personnel for the New Diplomacy*. Washington, D.C.: Carnegie Endowment For International Peace, 1962.

Report of the Rocky Mountain Assembly. *The Secretary of State*. Provo, Utah: Brigham Young University, 1961.

Steiner, Zara S. *Present Problems of the Foreign Service*. Princeton, New Jersey: Princeton University, 1961.

UNPUBLISHED MATERIALS

Rosenau, James N. "The Senate and Dean Acheson: A Case Study in Legislative Attitudes." Unpublished Ph.D. Thesis. Princeton, New Jersey: Princeton University, 1957.

Schonhaut, Beatrice May. "Secretary Acheson's China Policy, January 1949–June 1950." Unpublished M.A. Thesis. Columbus, Ohio: The Ohio State University, 1965.

Stupak, Ronald J. "British Labor Party Policy and Attitudes Toward NATO and Western Defense." Unpublished M.A. Thesis, Columbus, Ohio: The Ohio State University, 1964.

Index